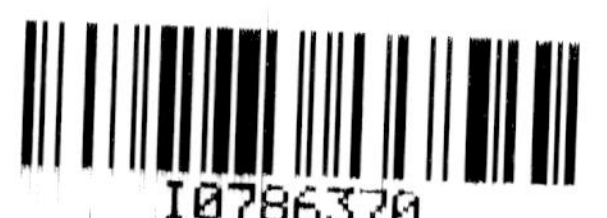

Beautiful Creatures: Grayscale Adult Coloring Books

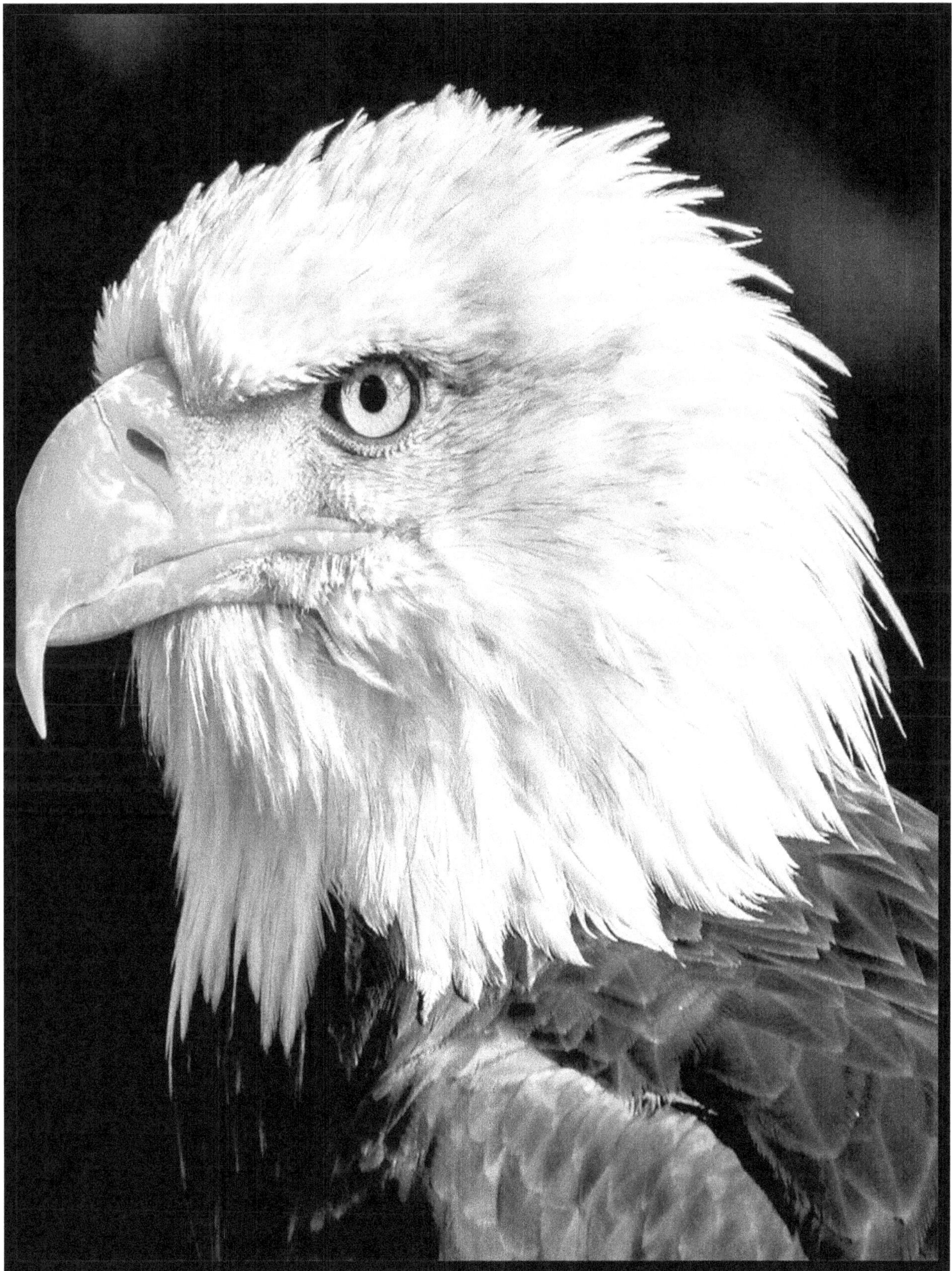

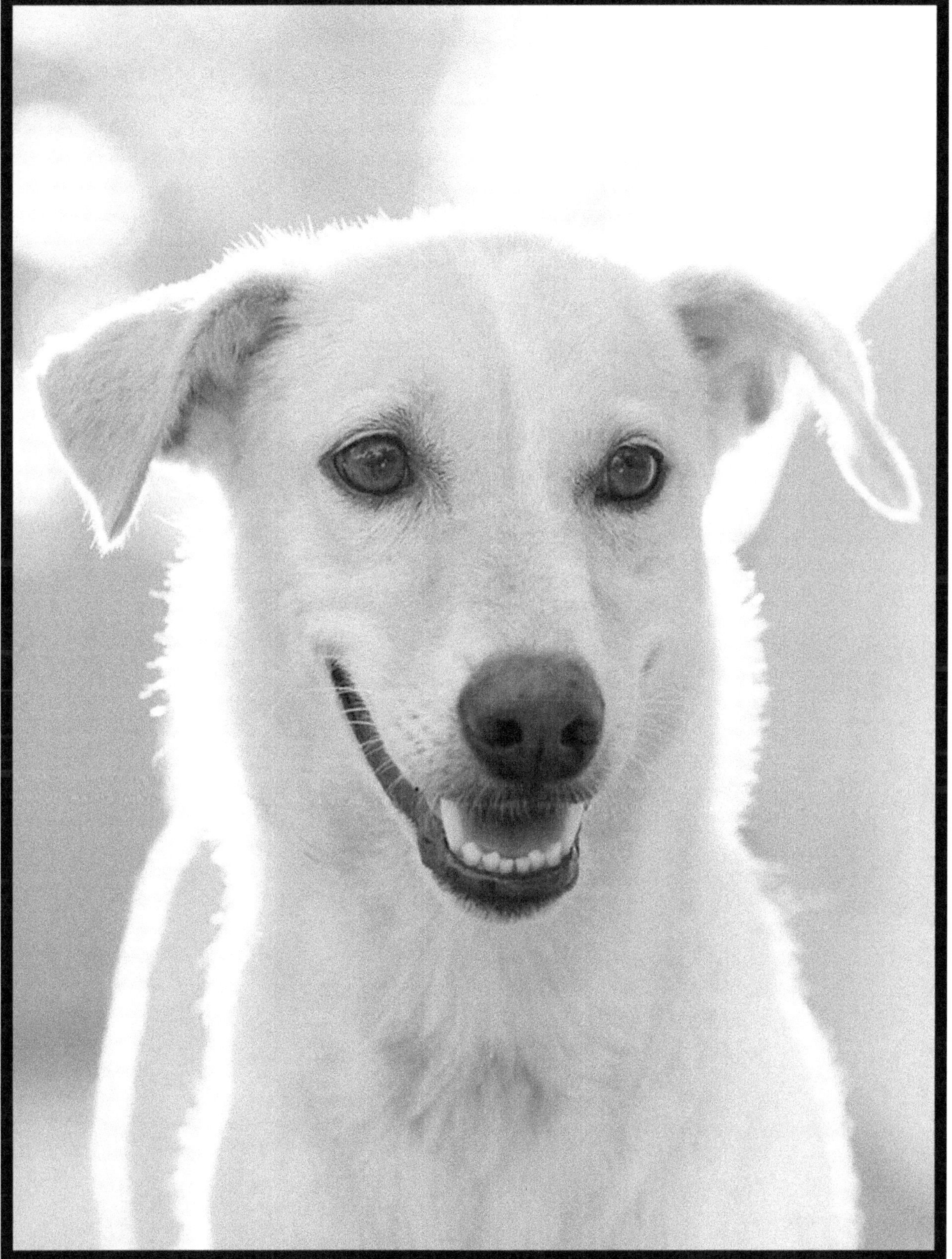

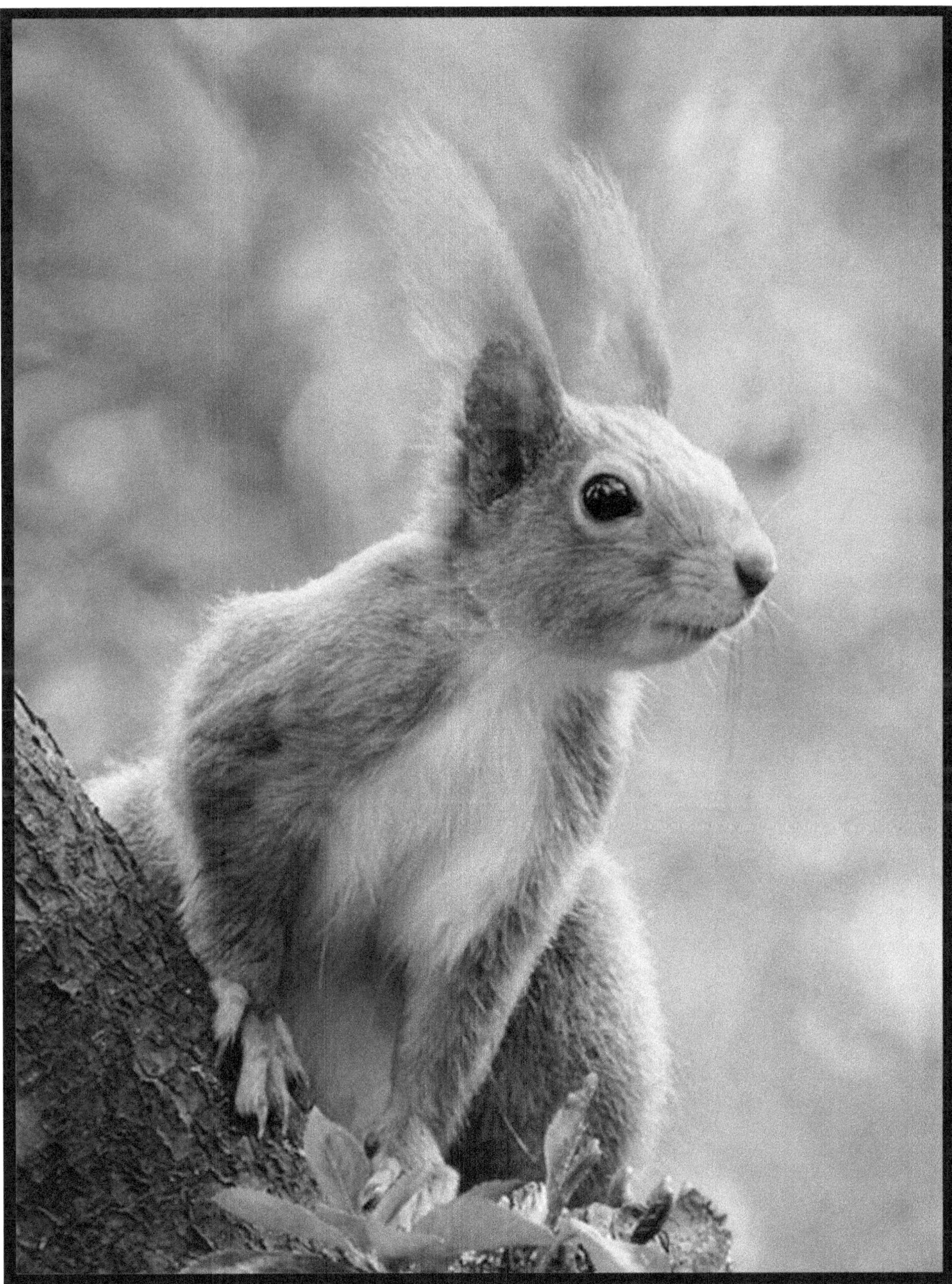

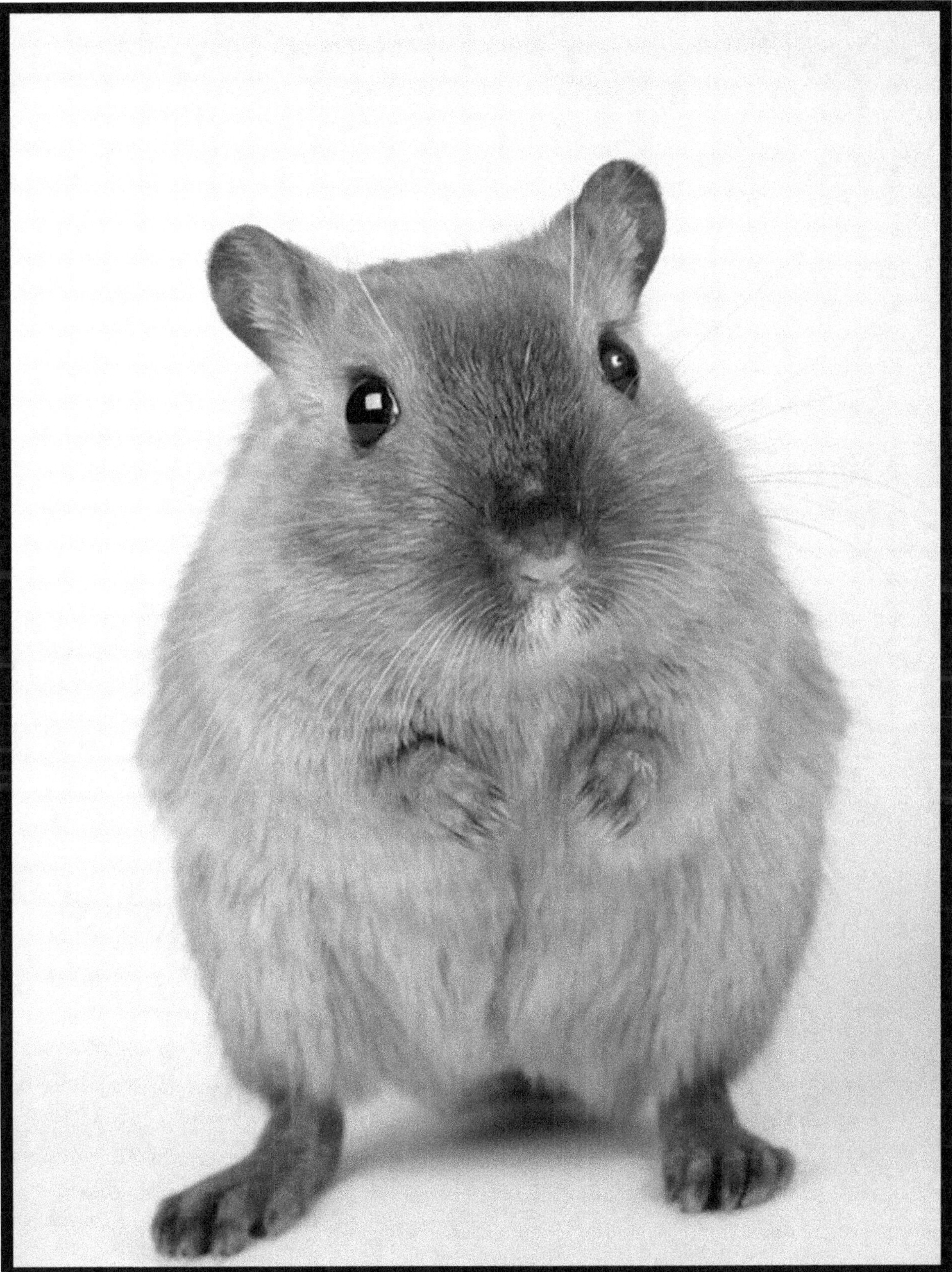

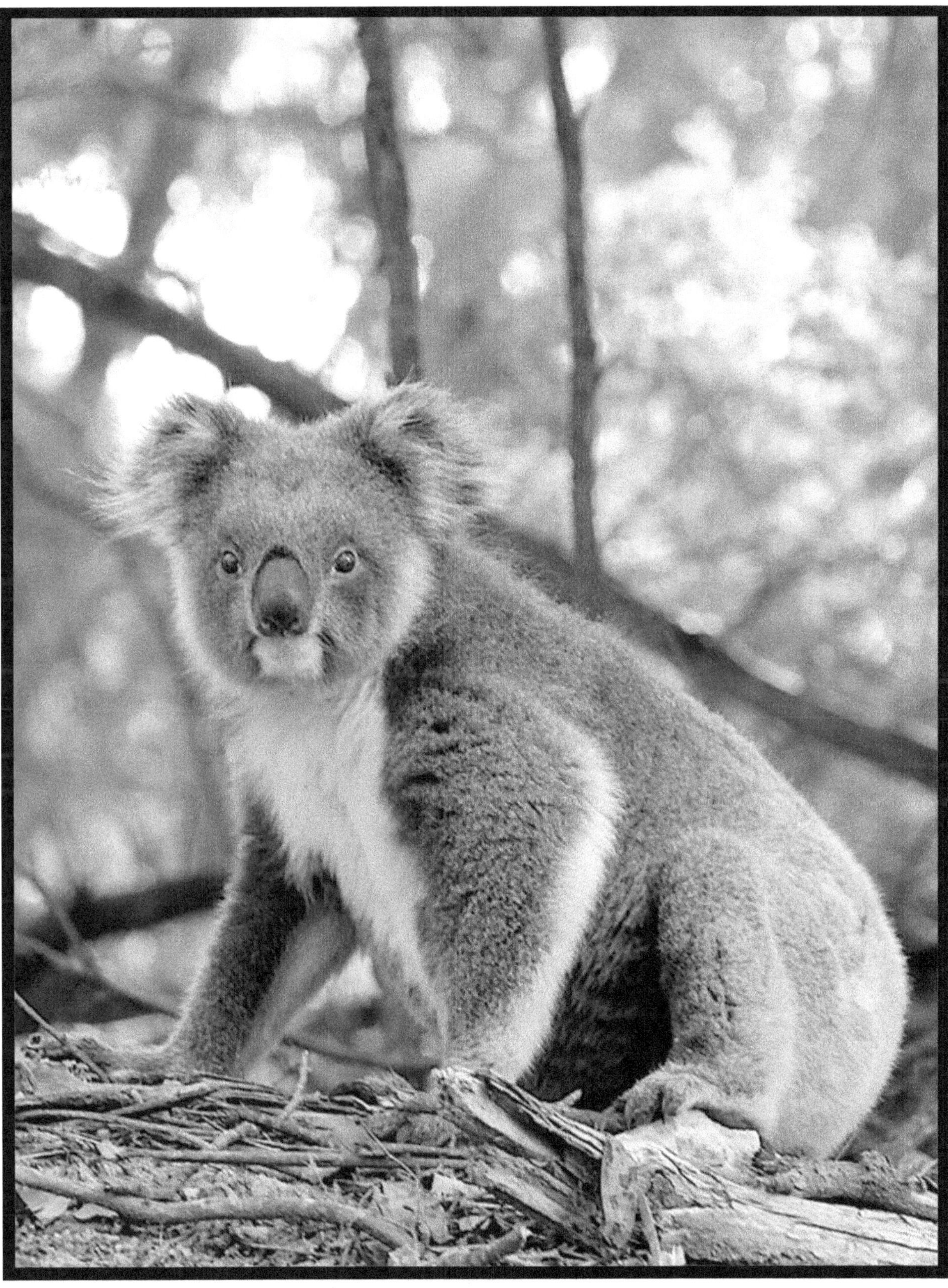

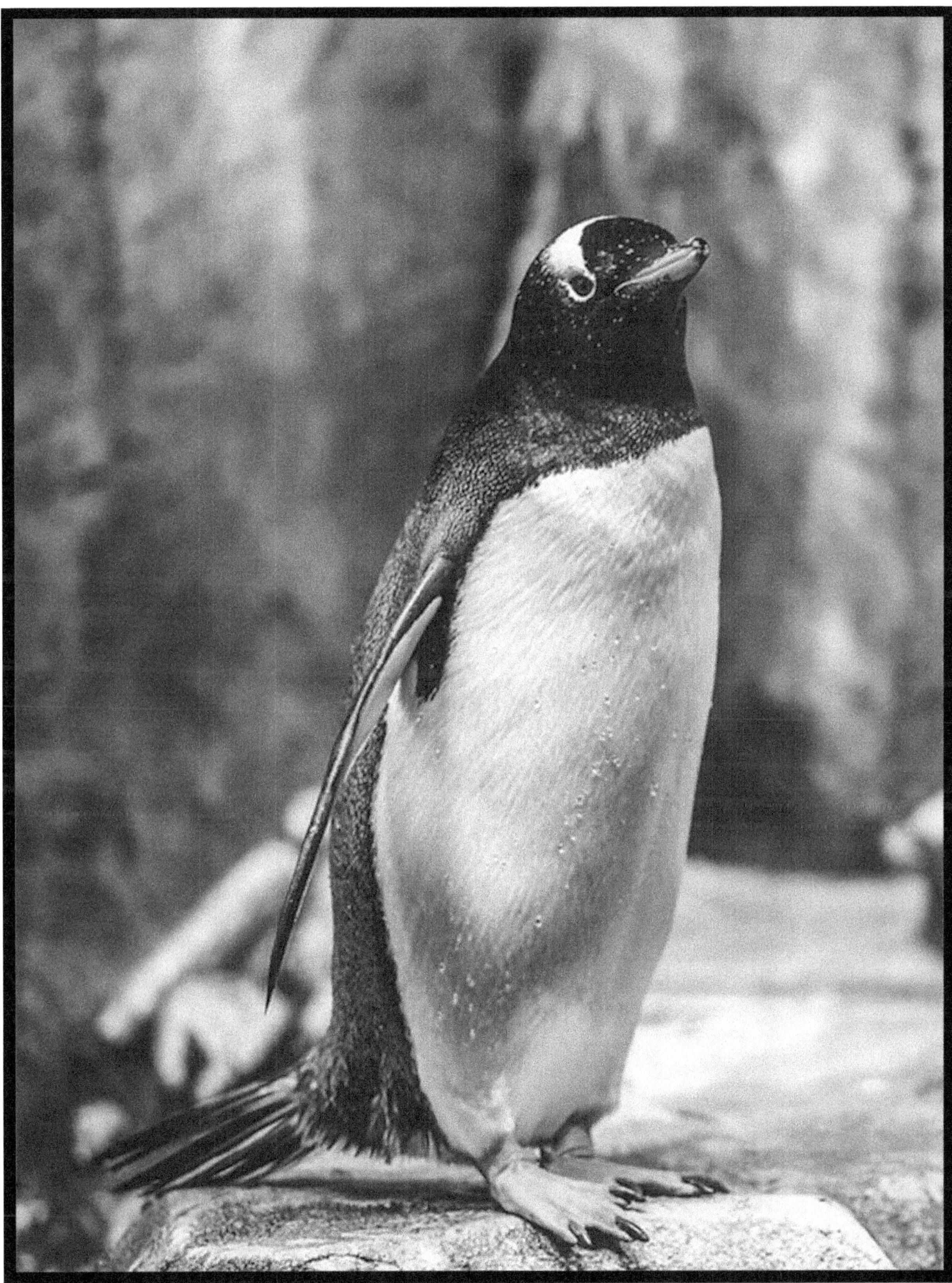

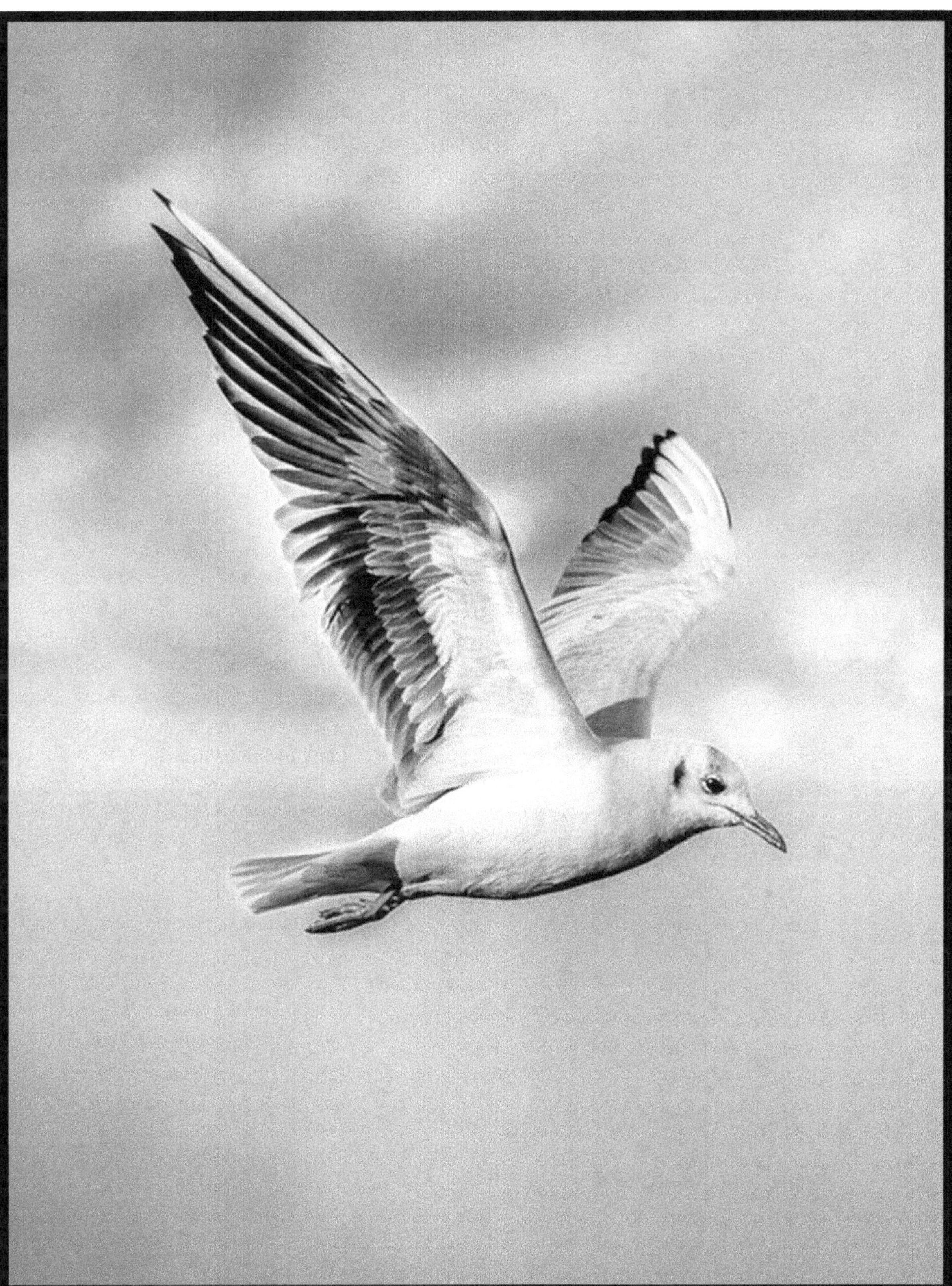

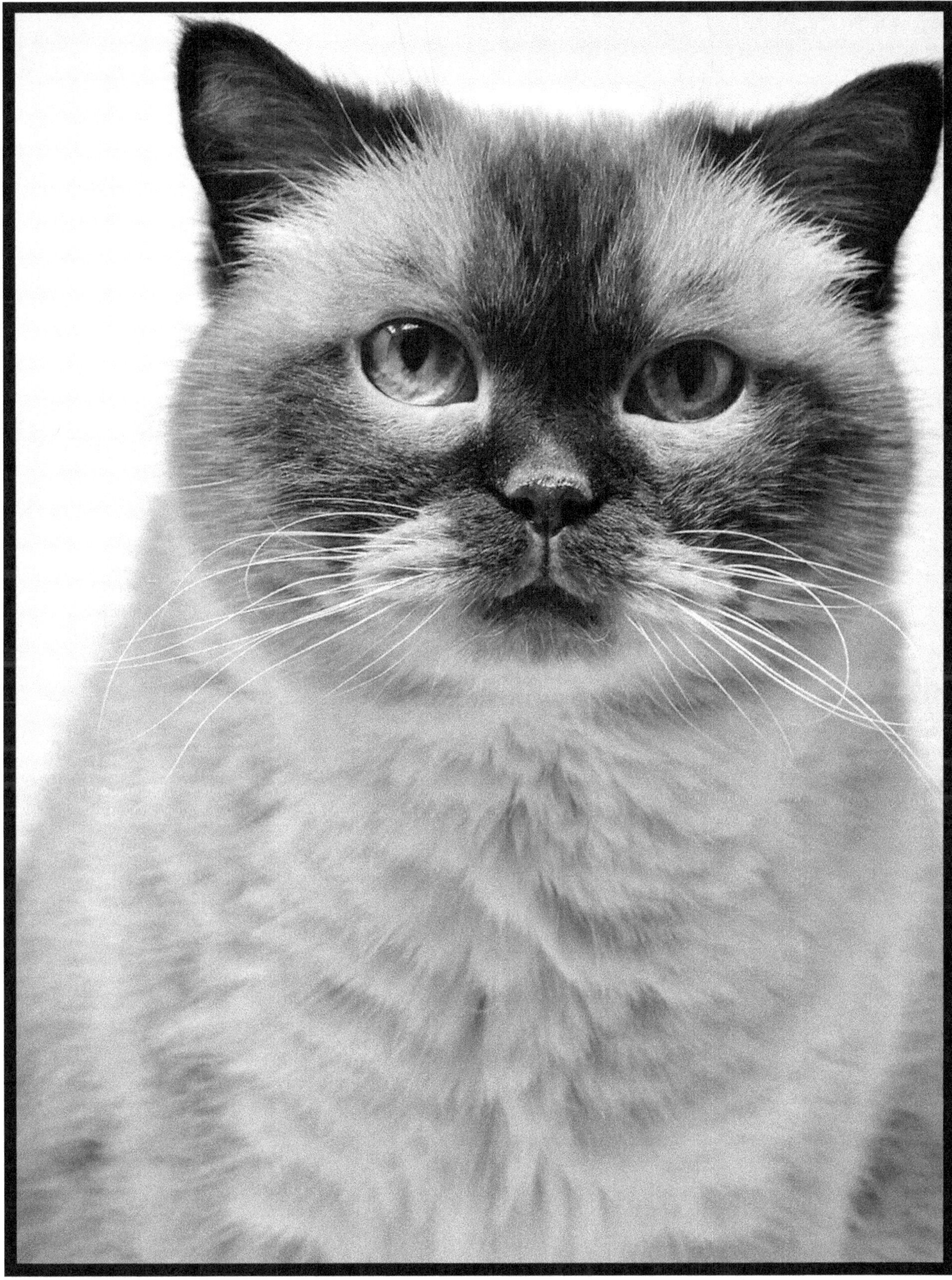

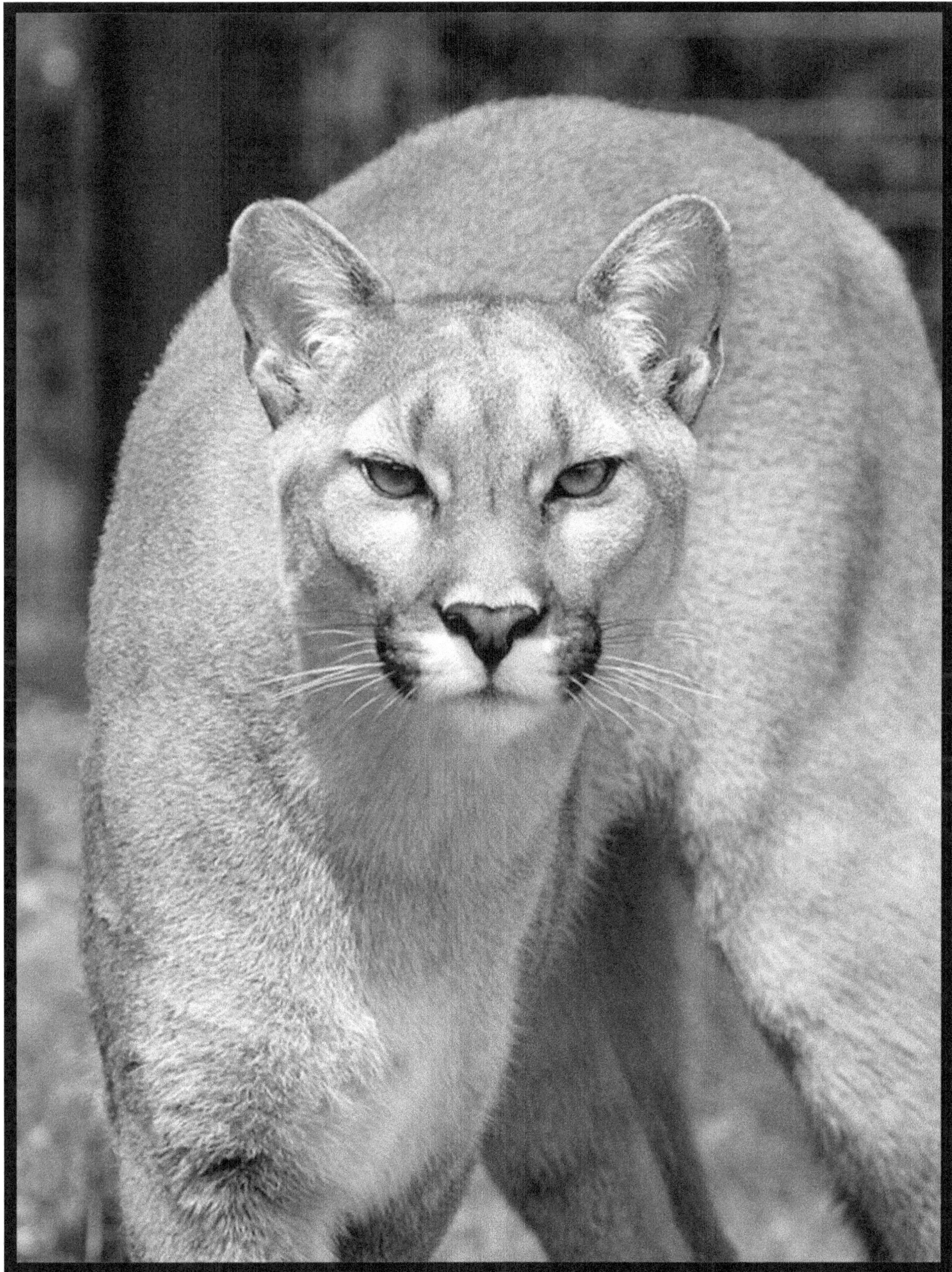

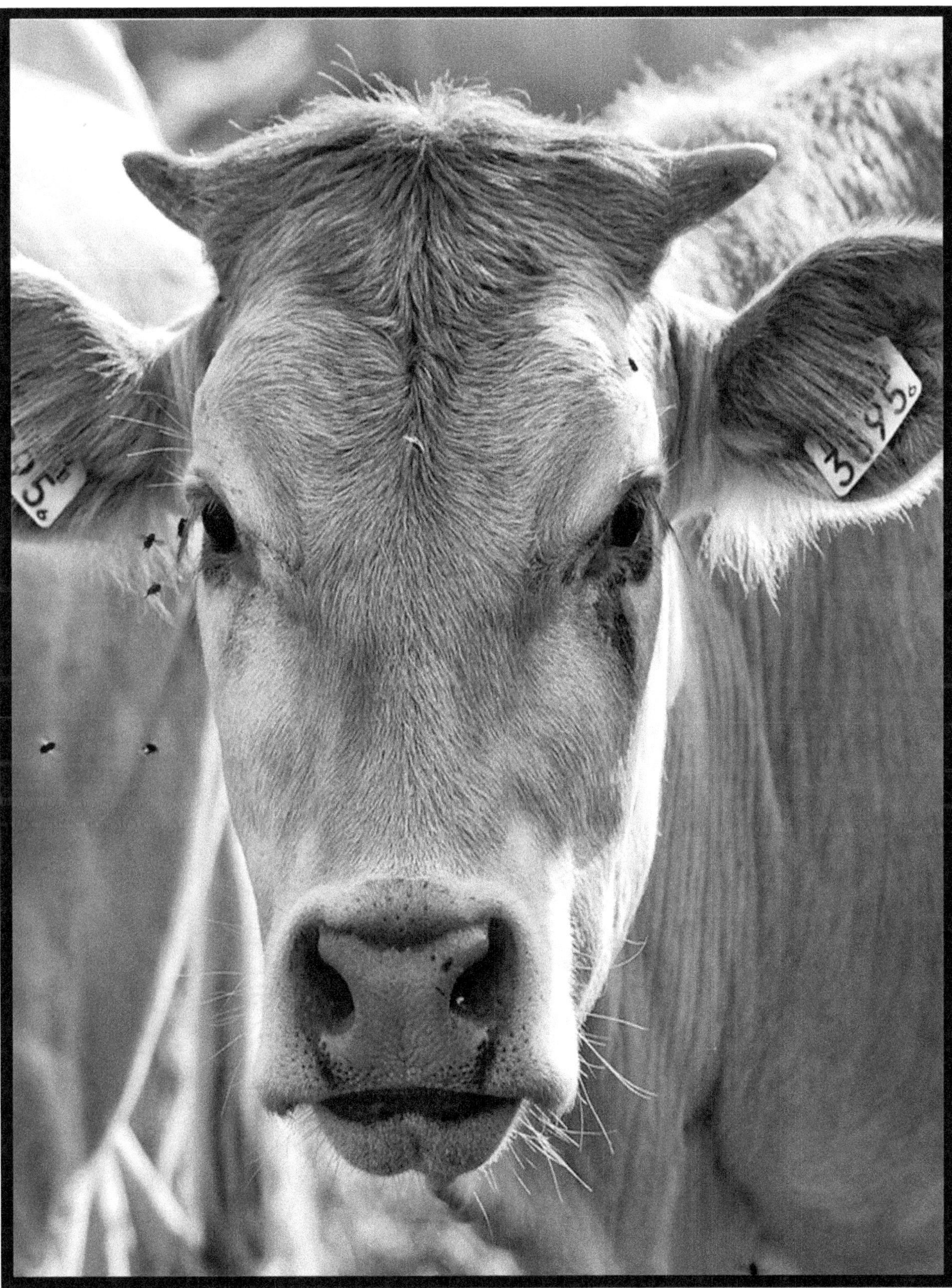

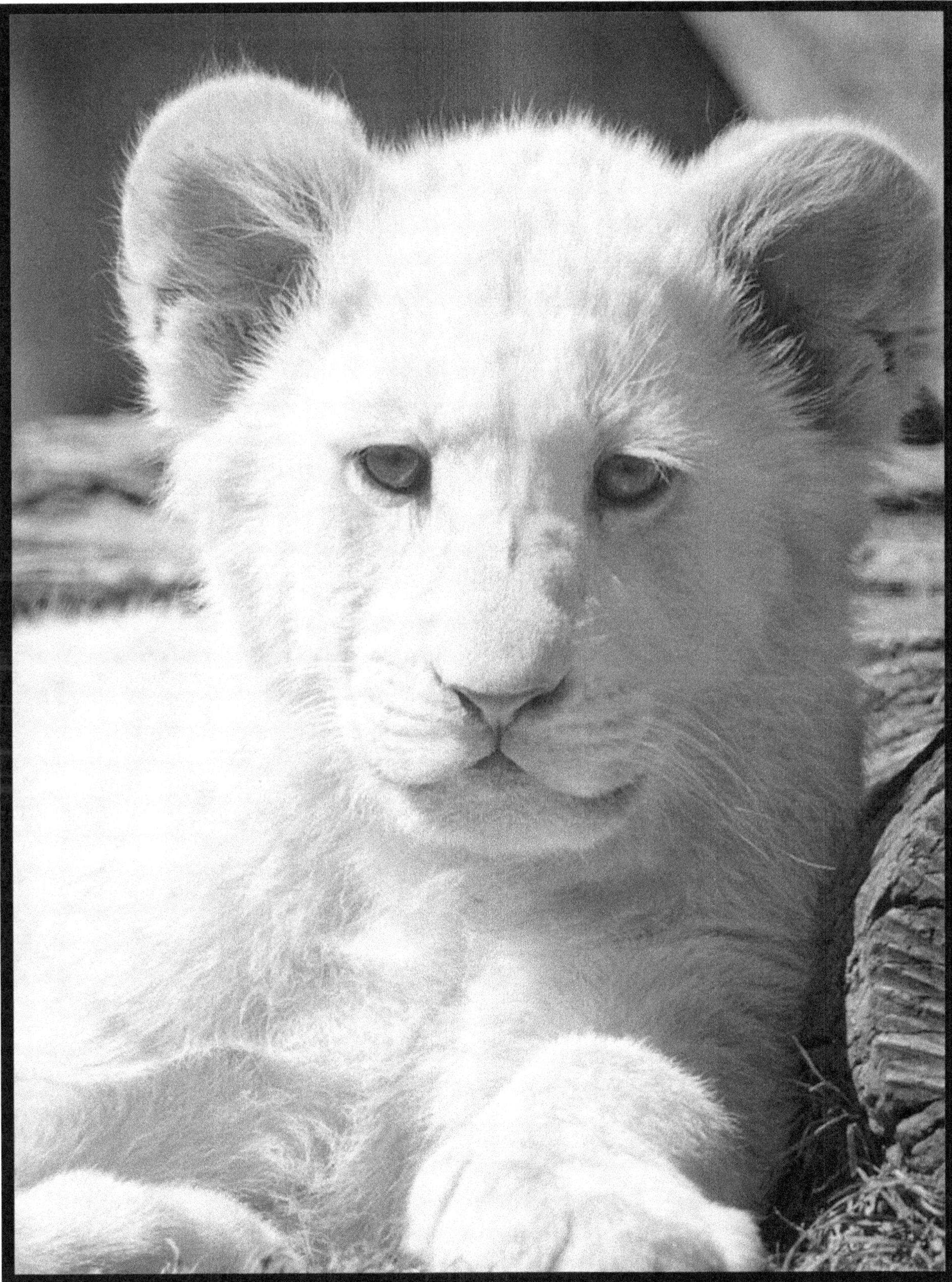

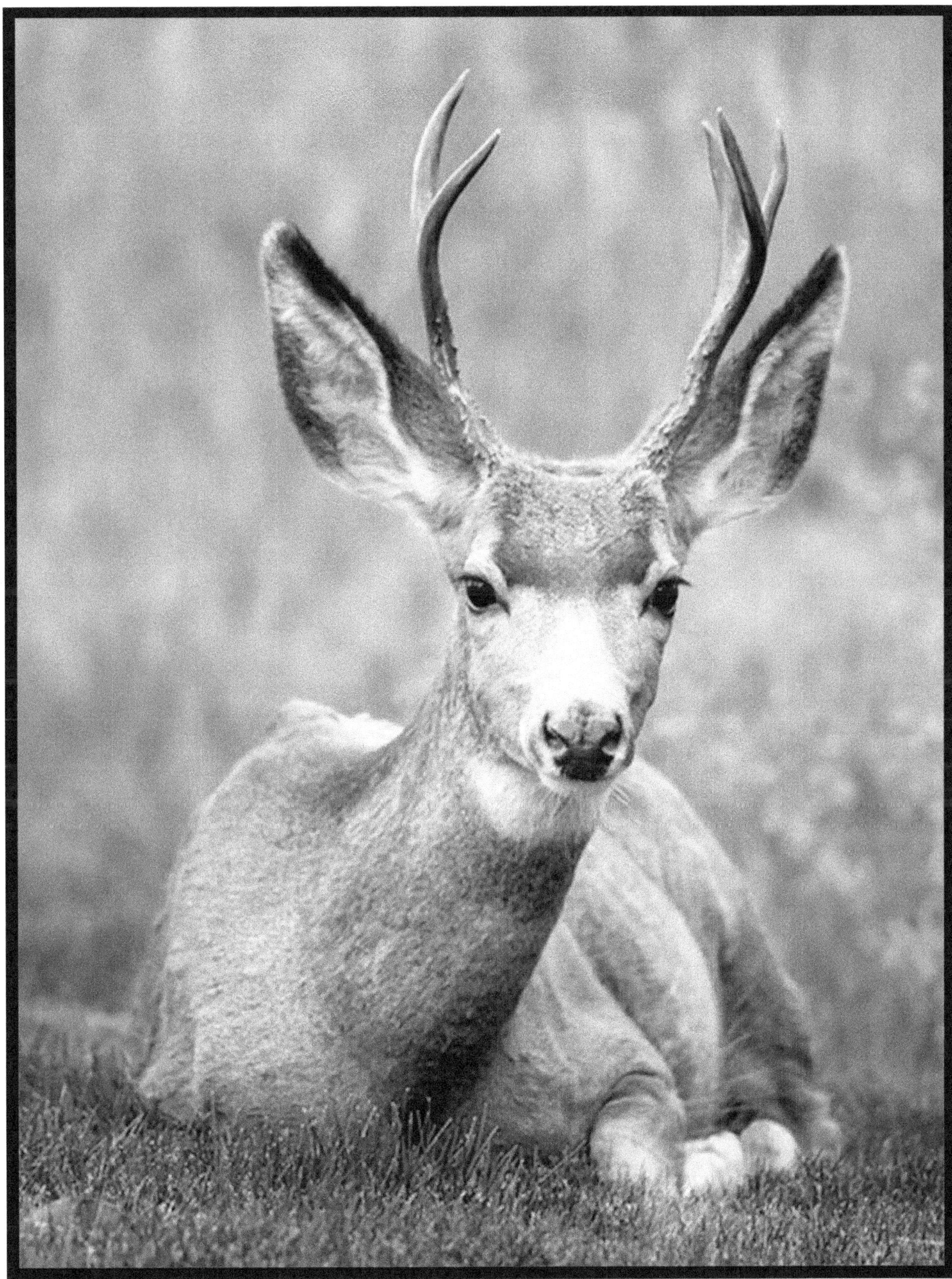

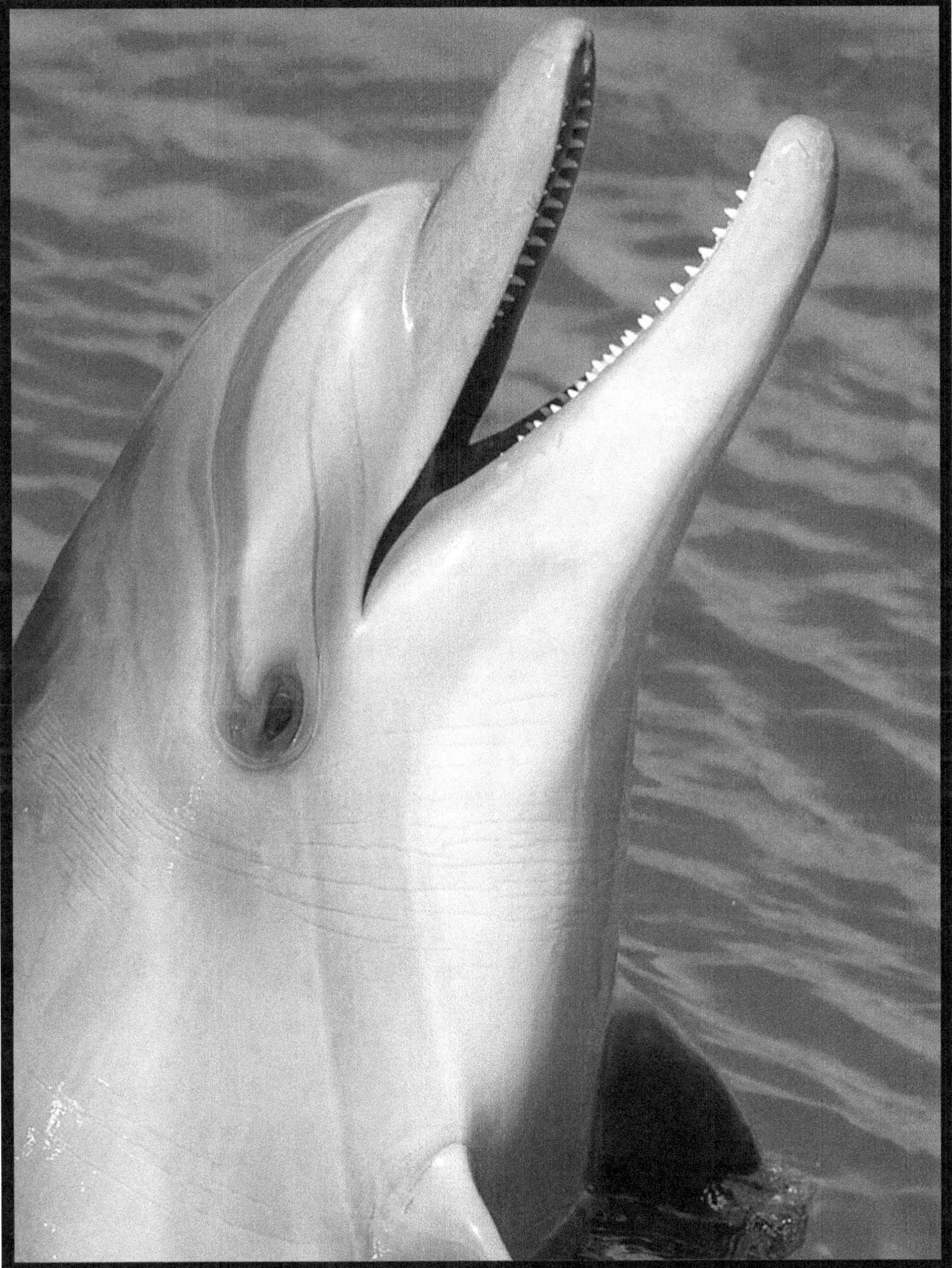

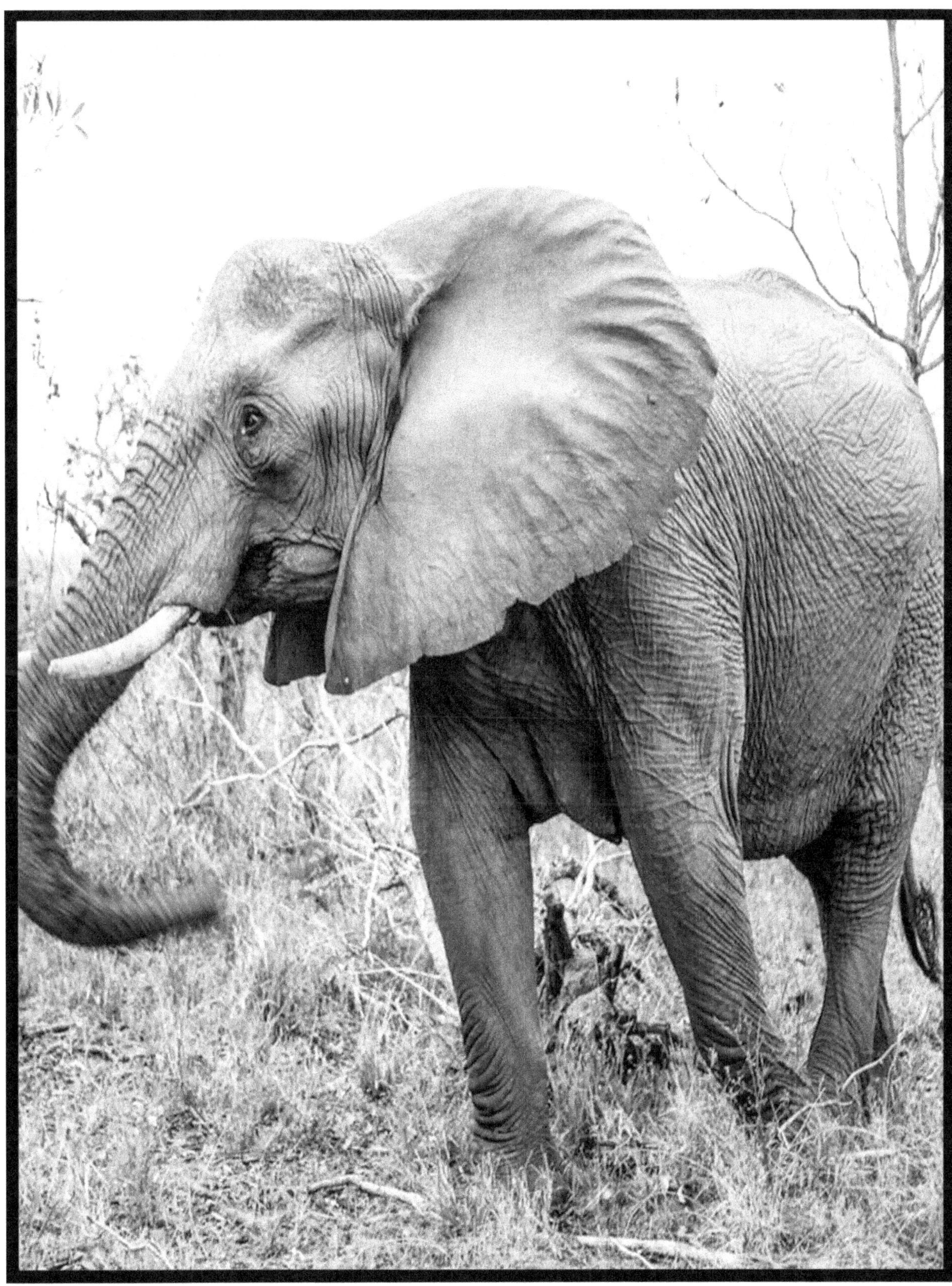

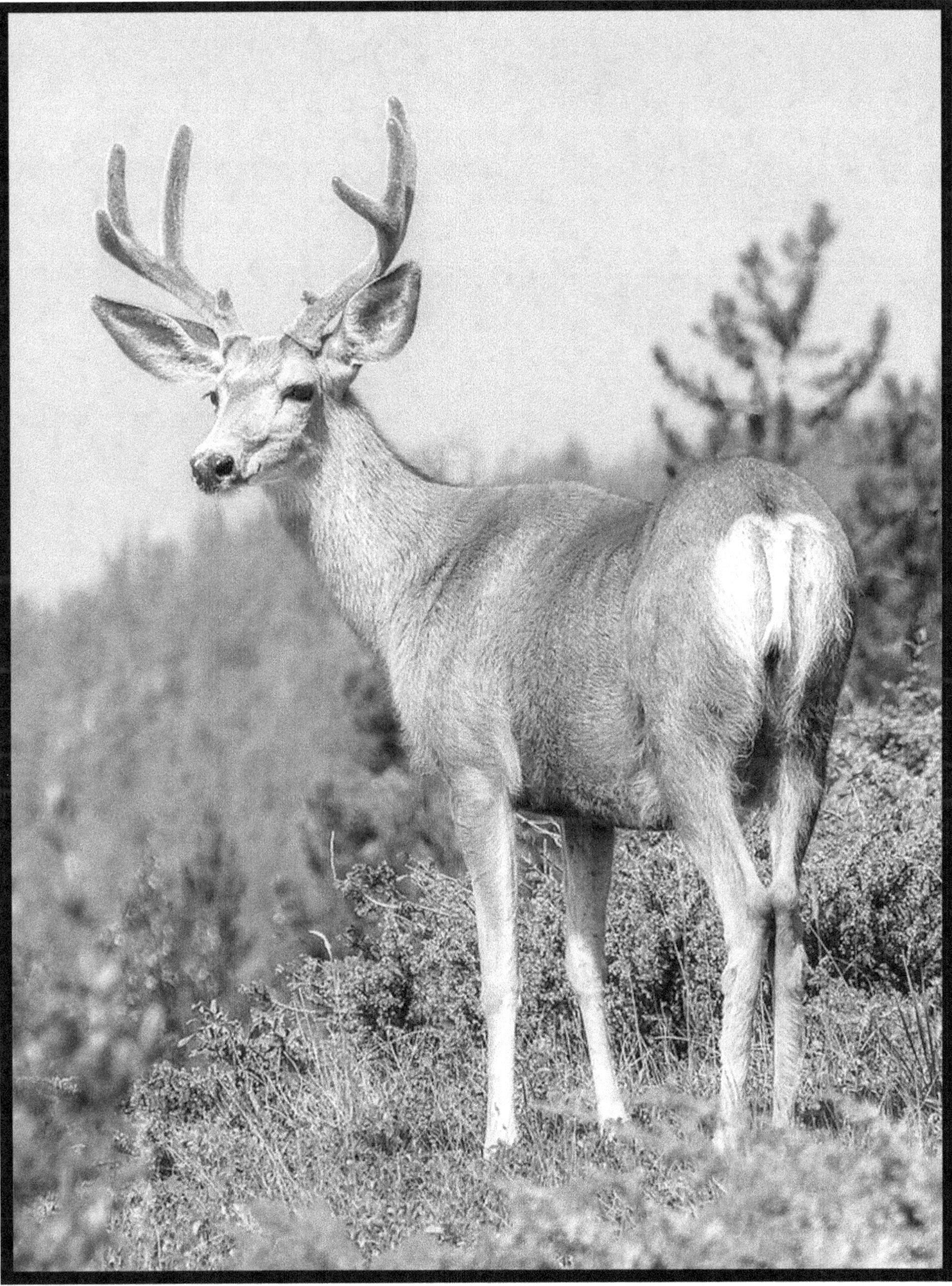

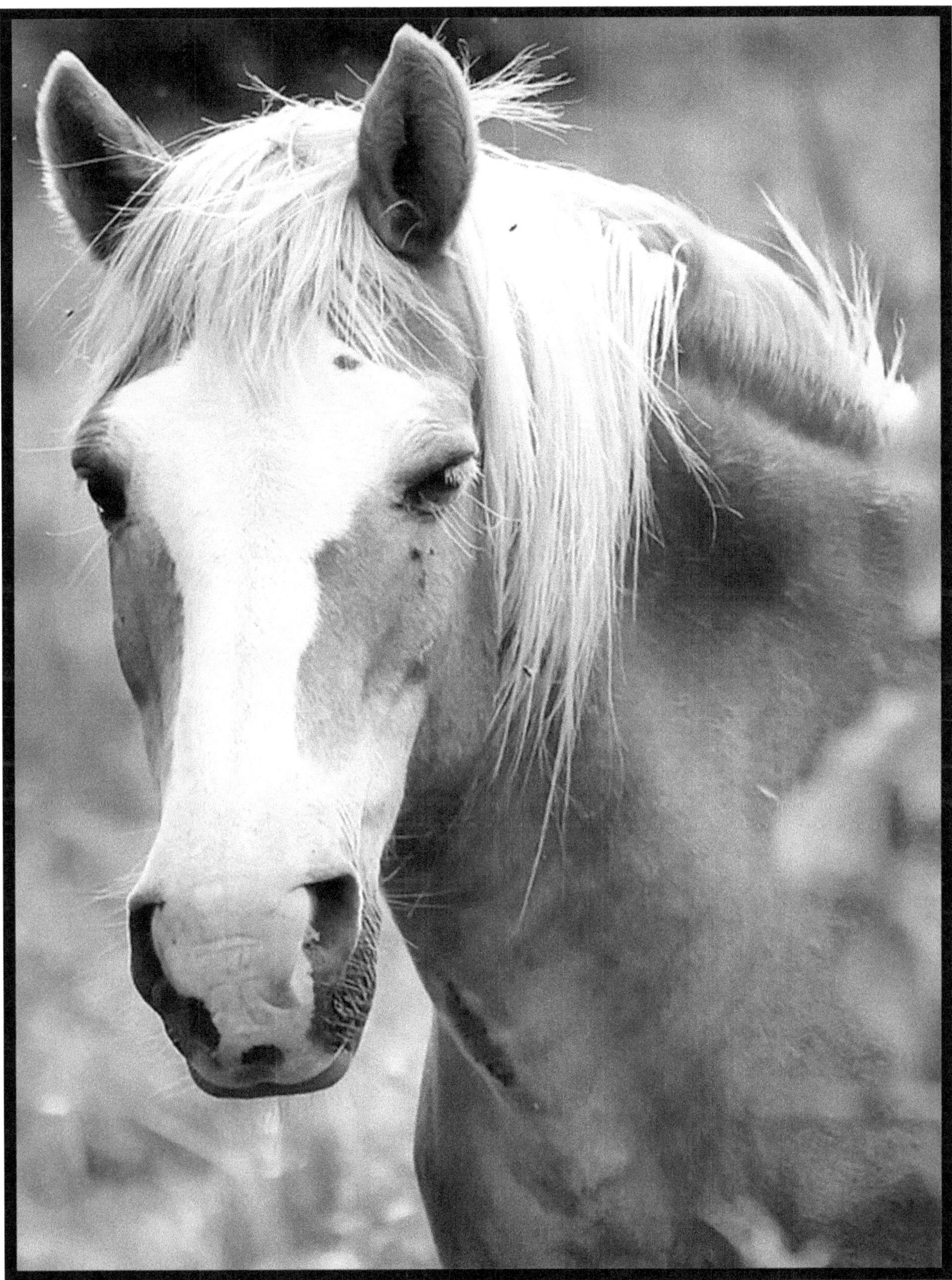

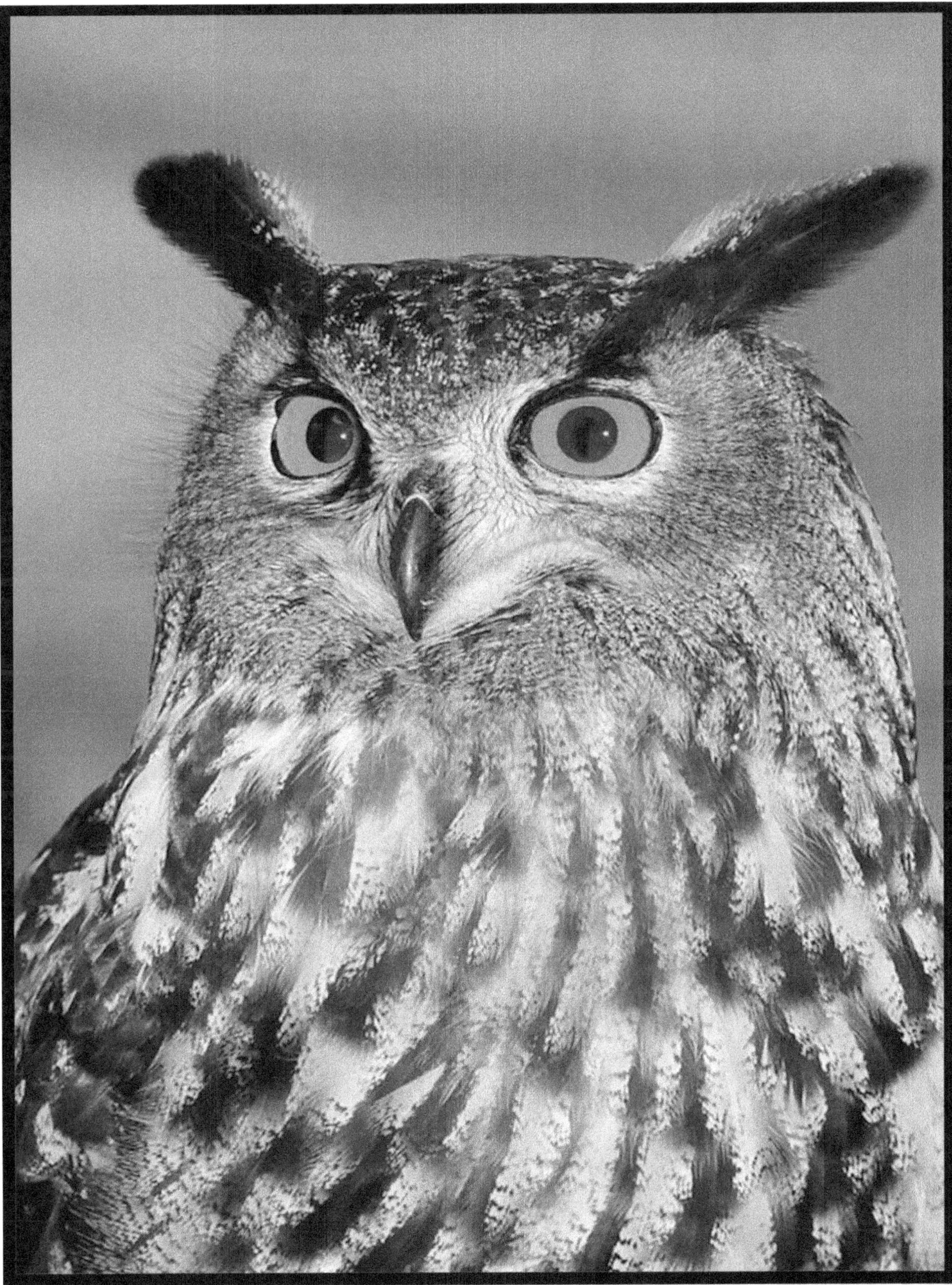

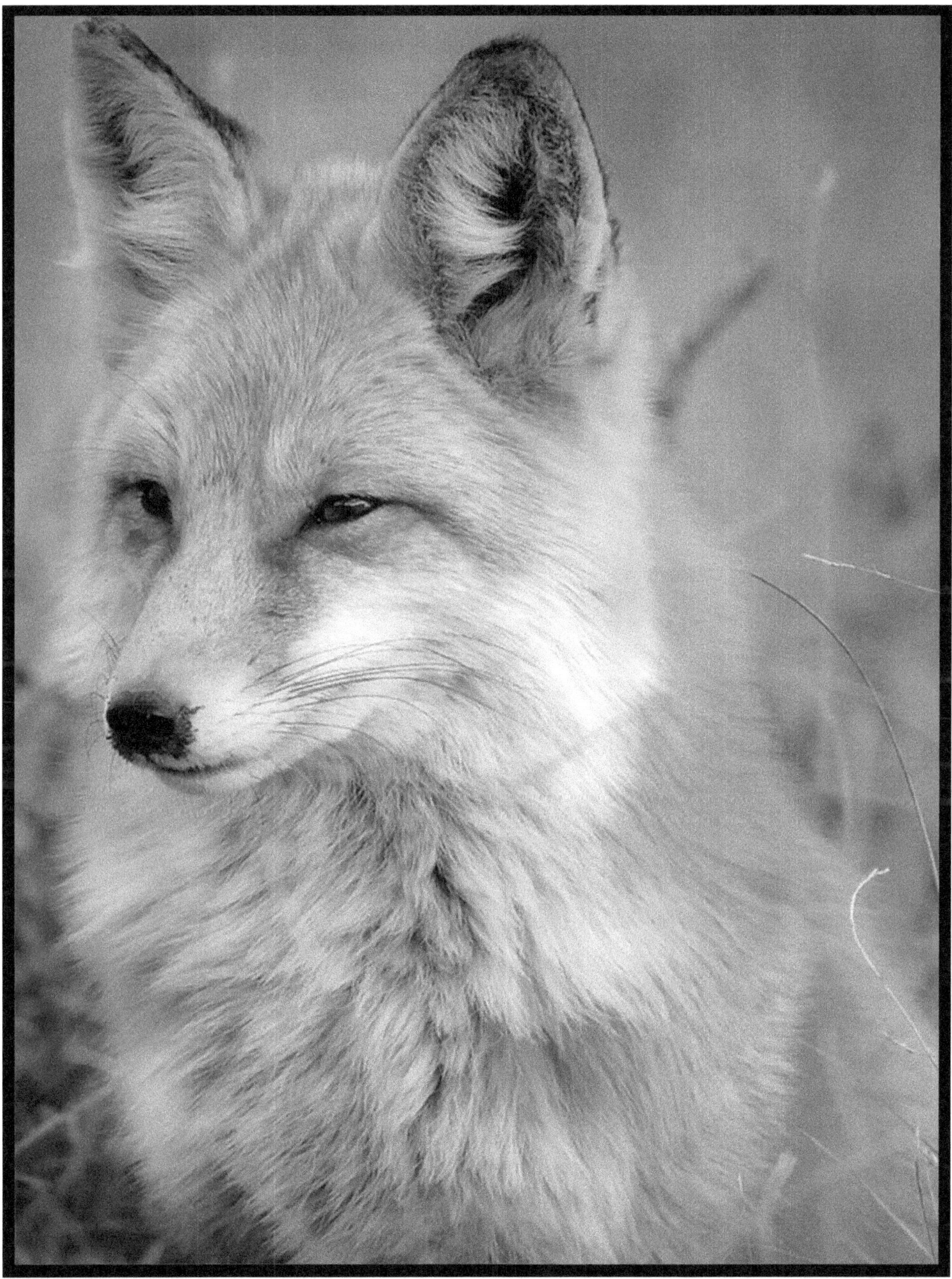

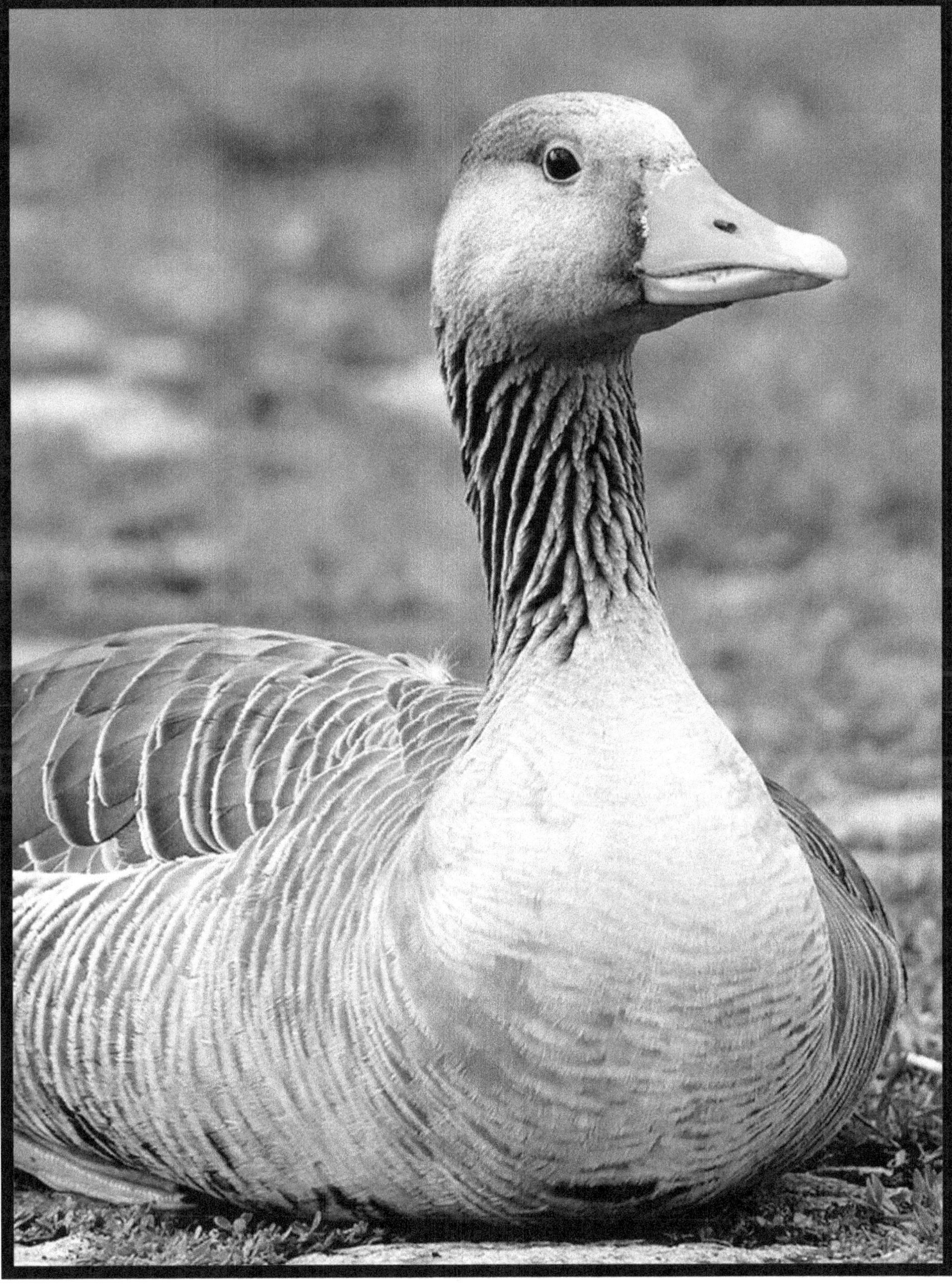

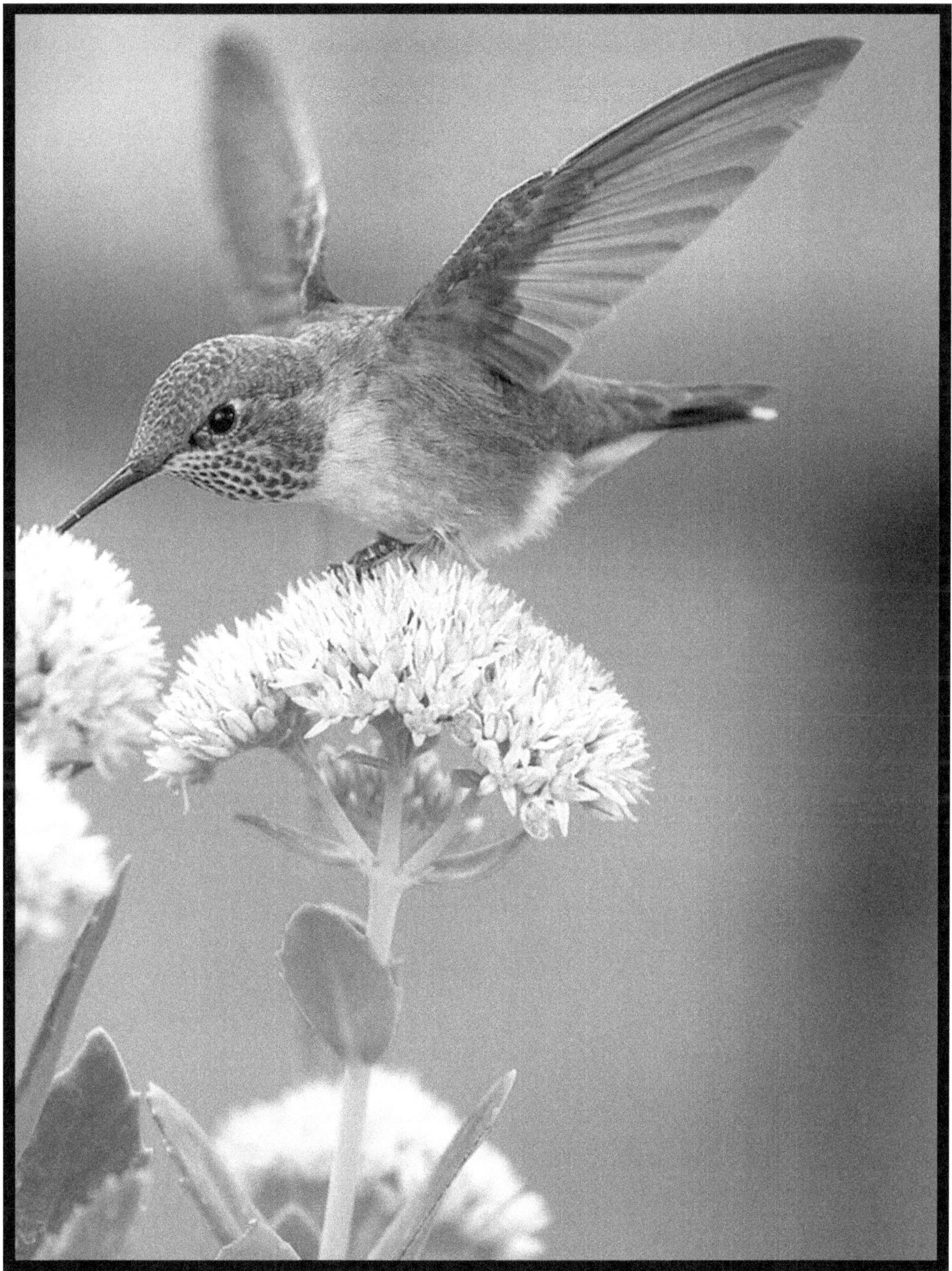

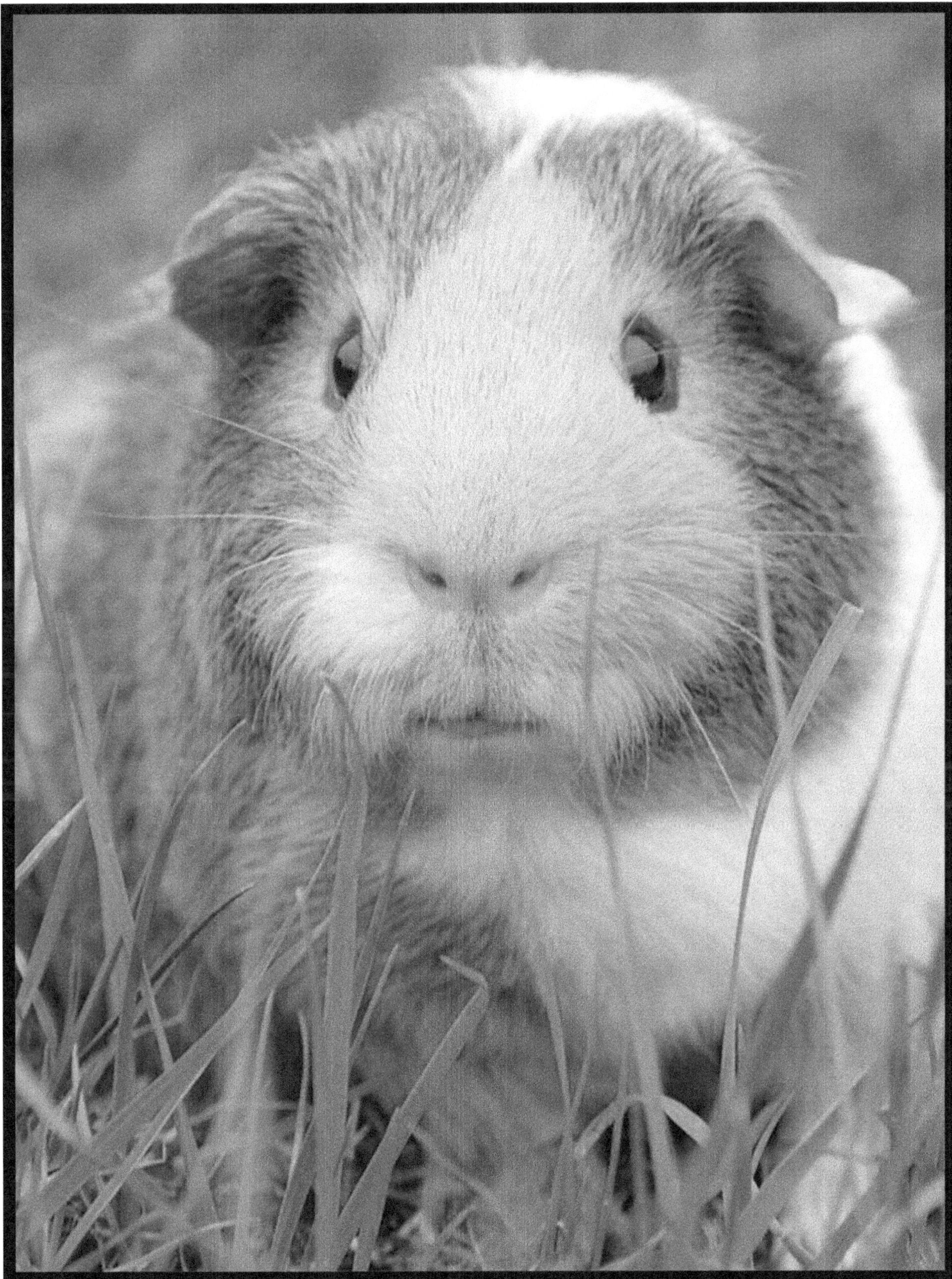

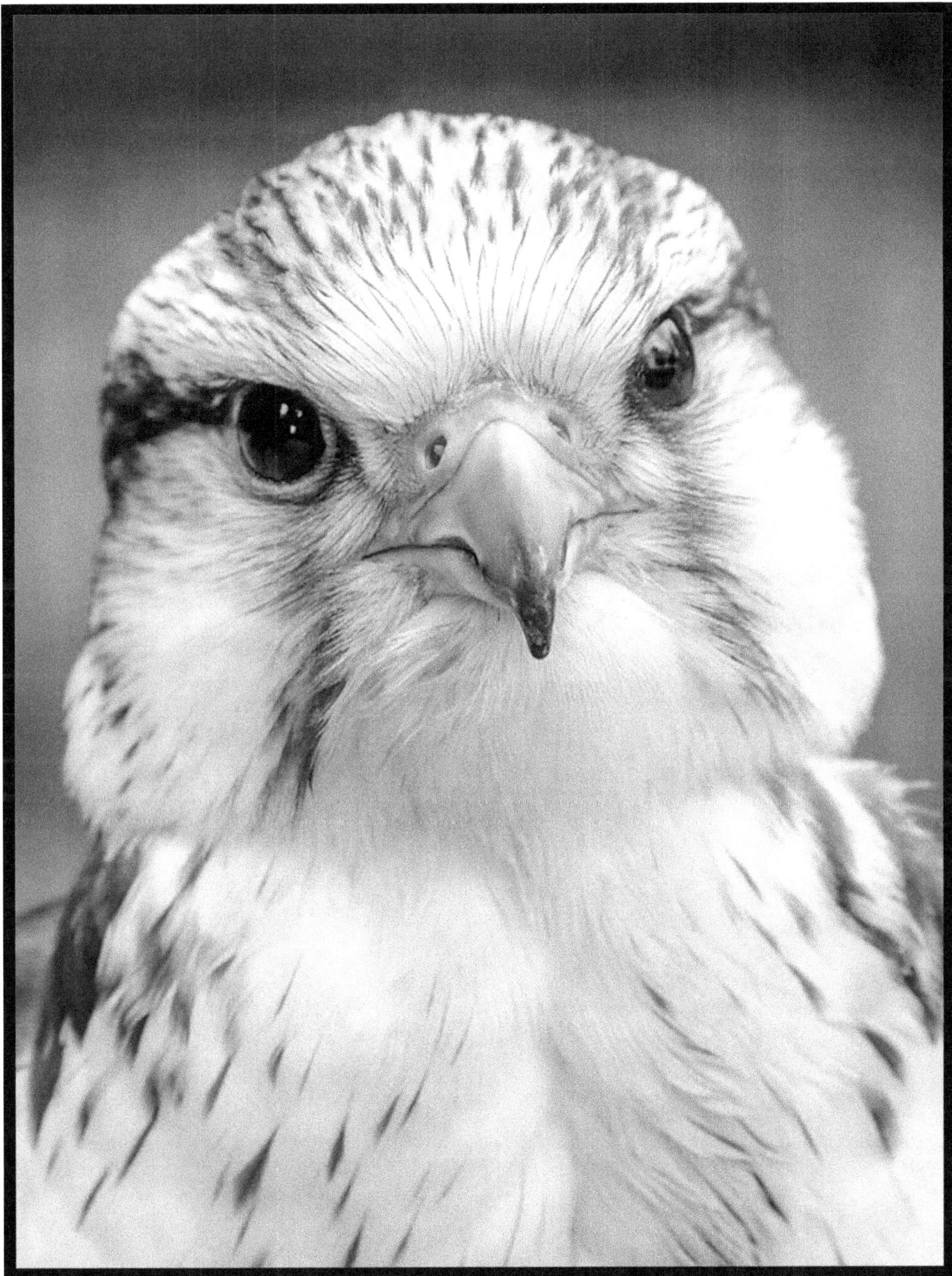

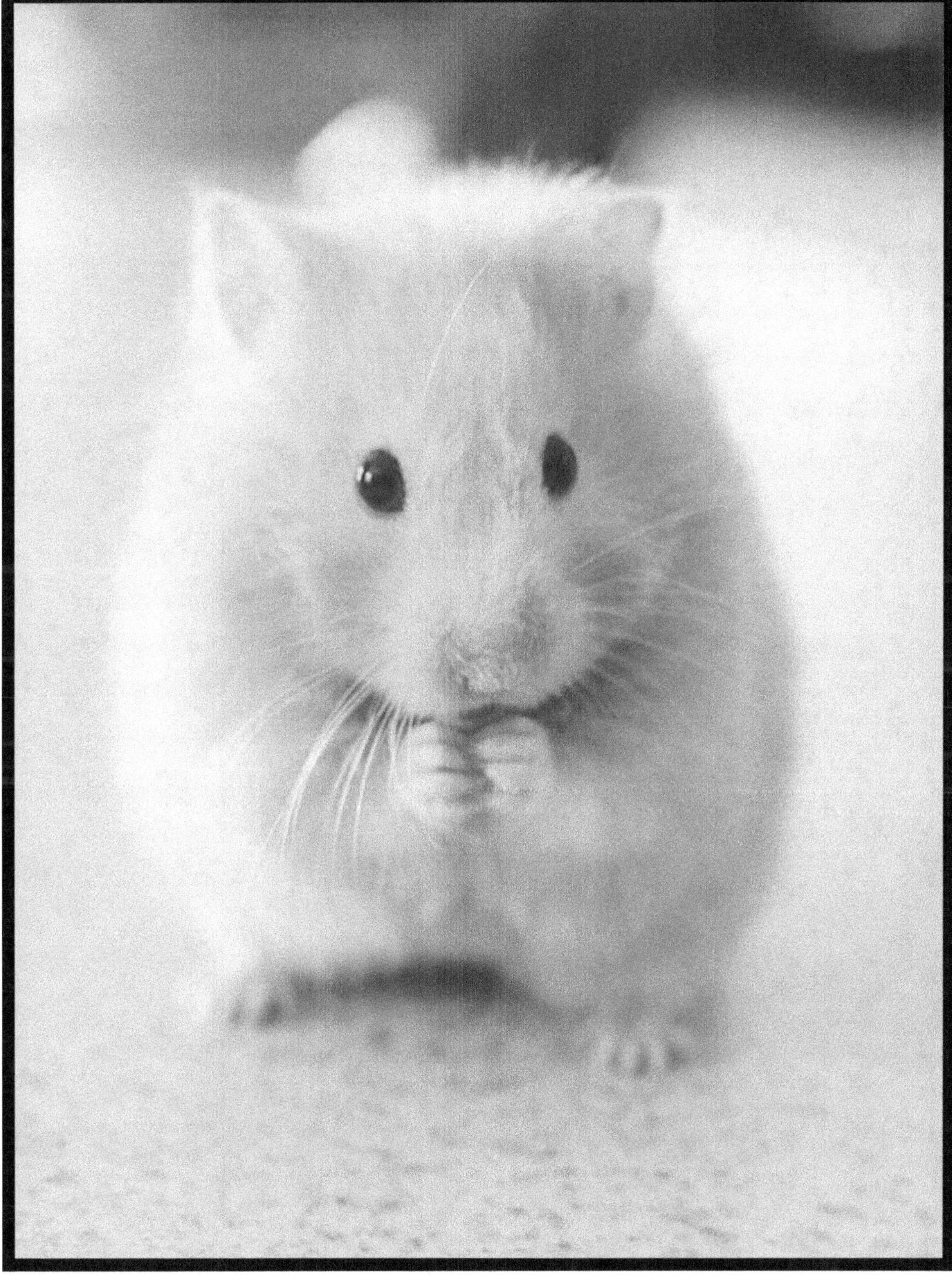

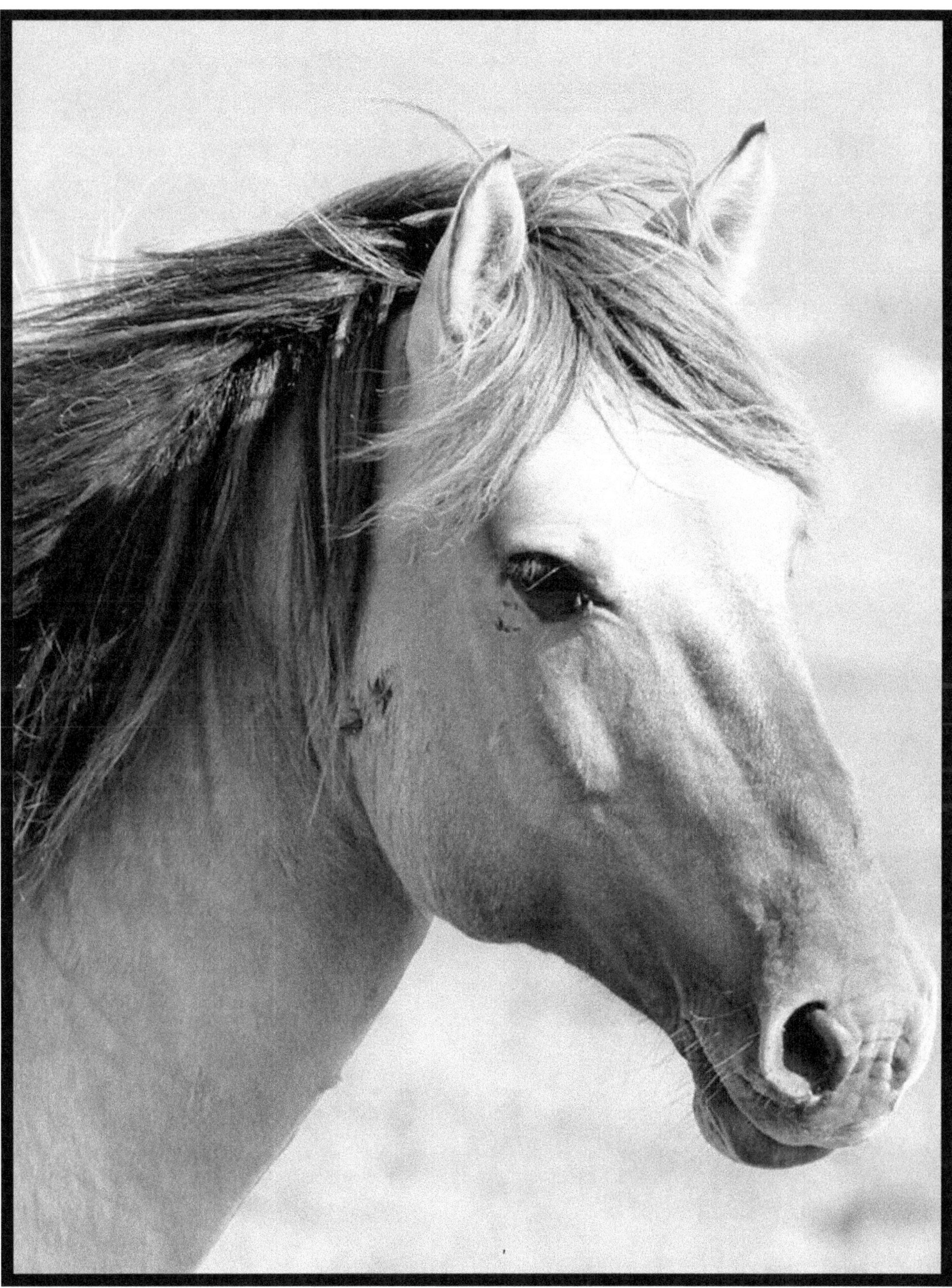

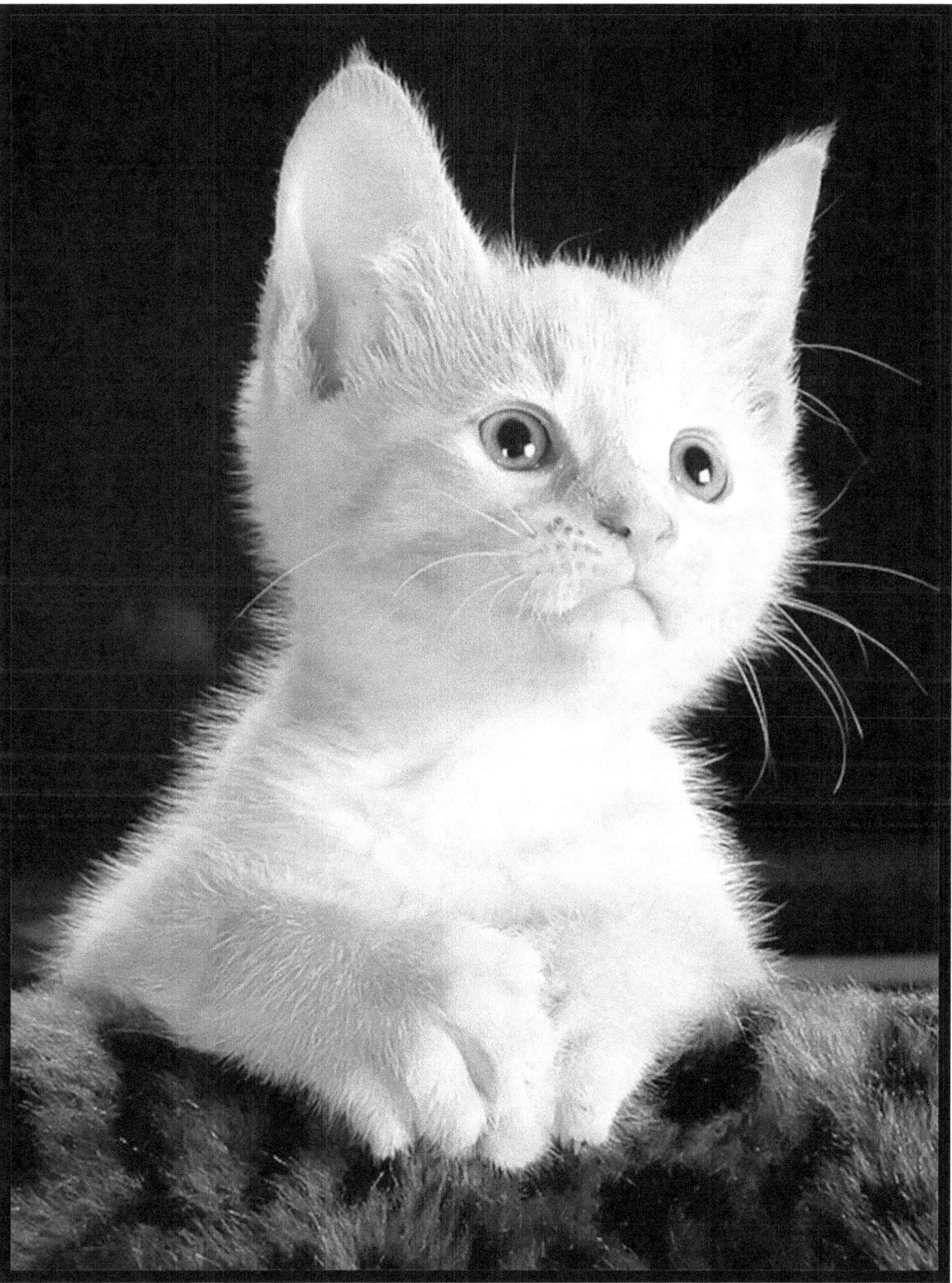

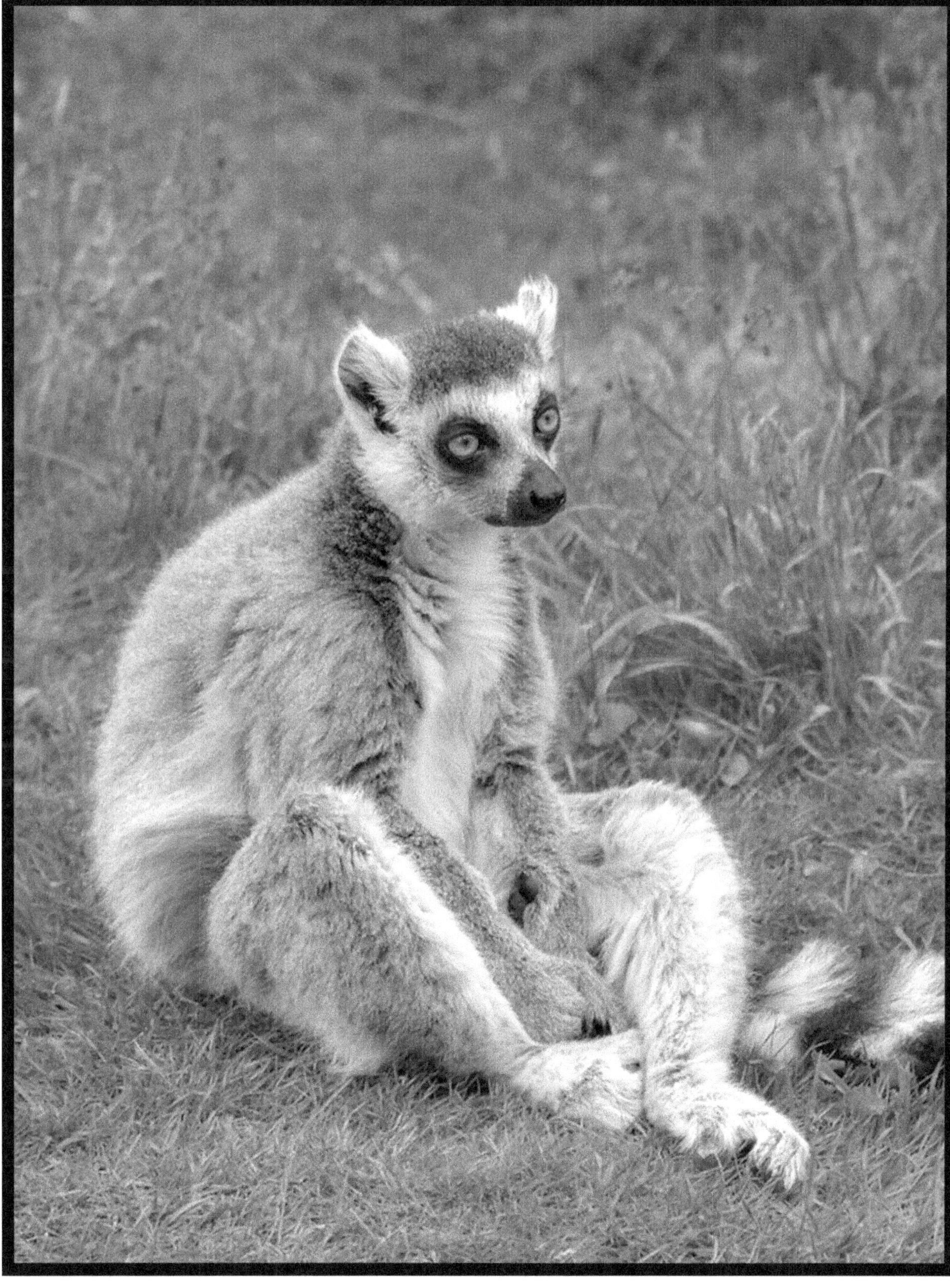

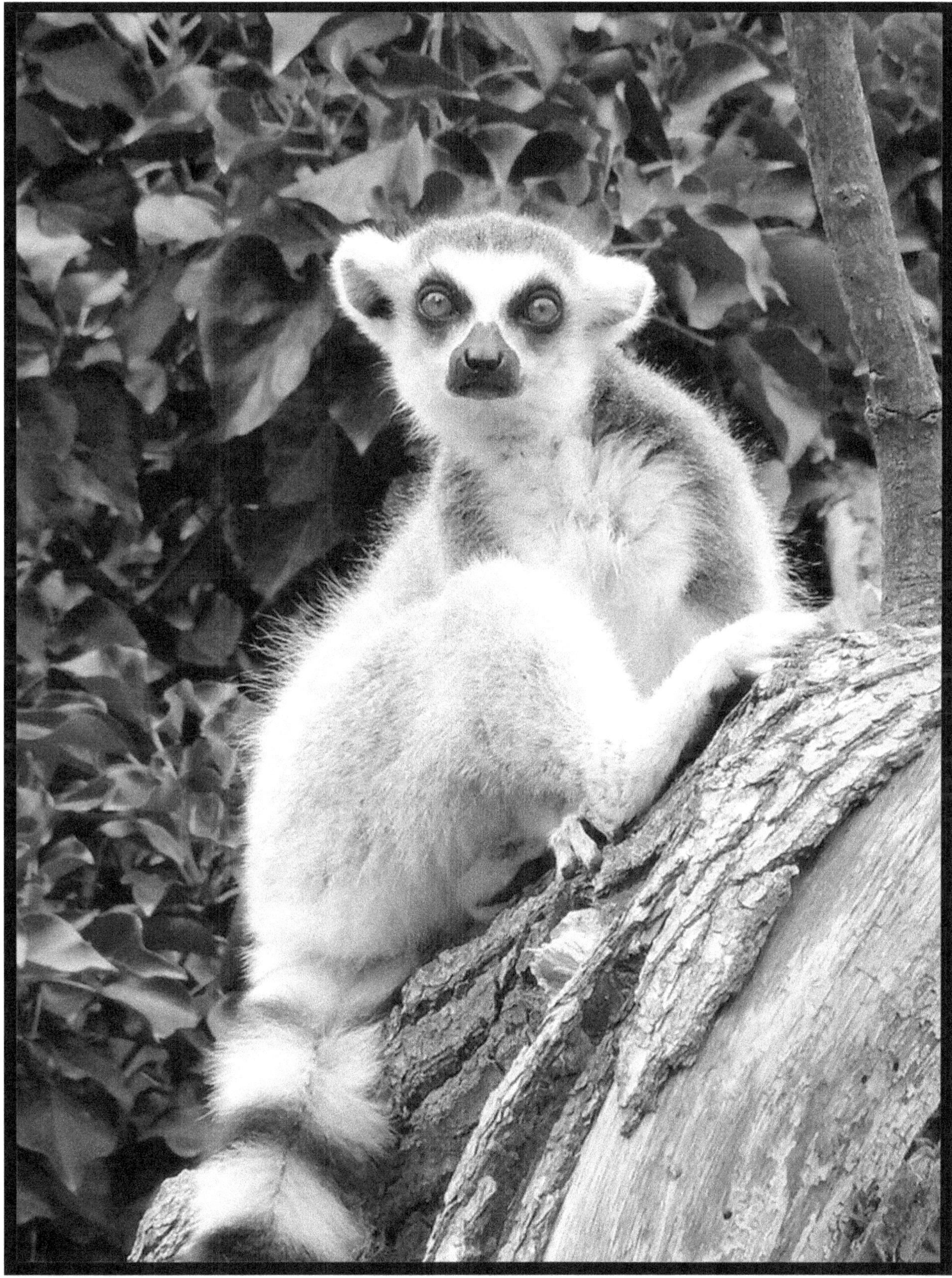

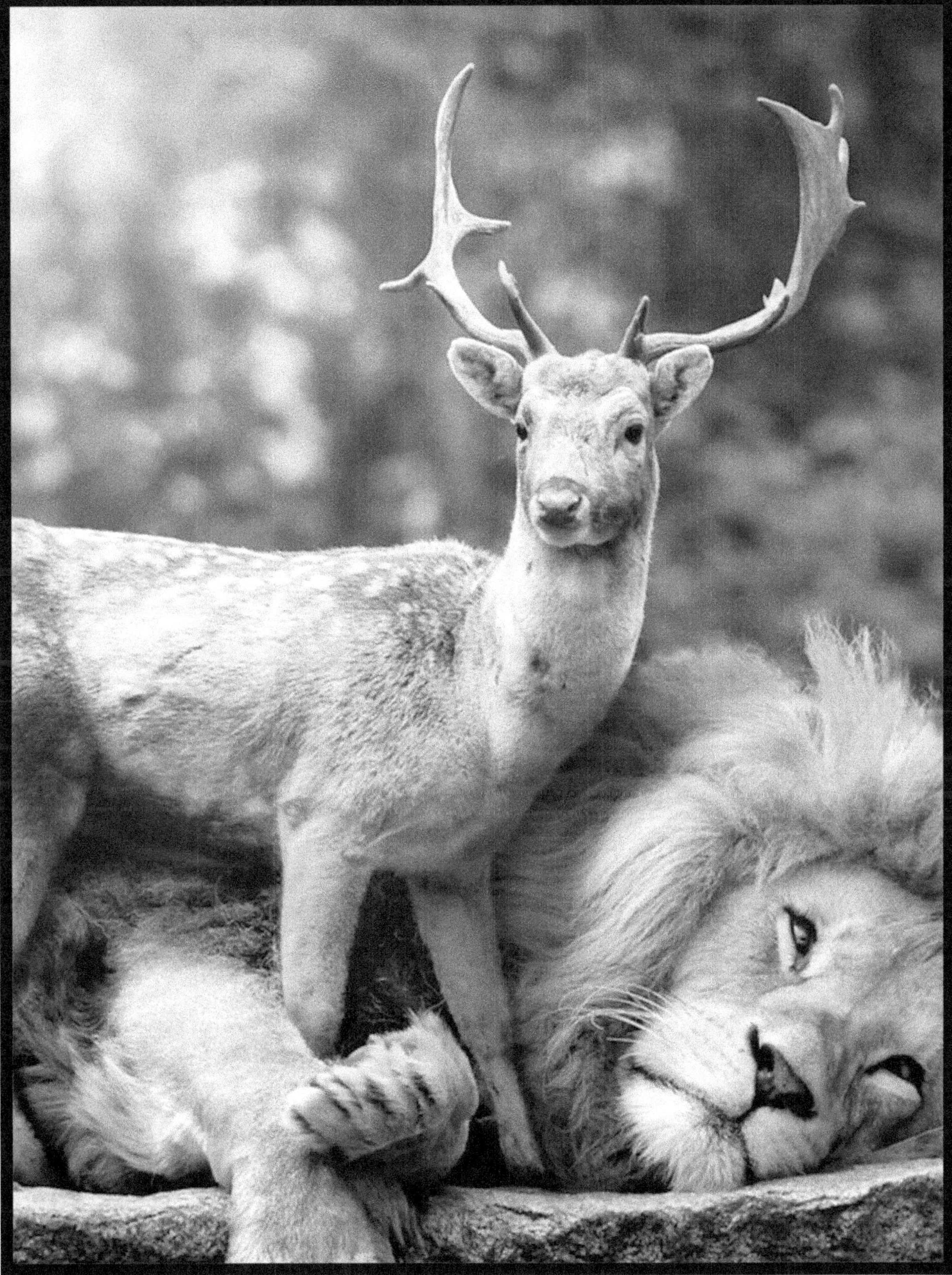

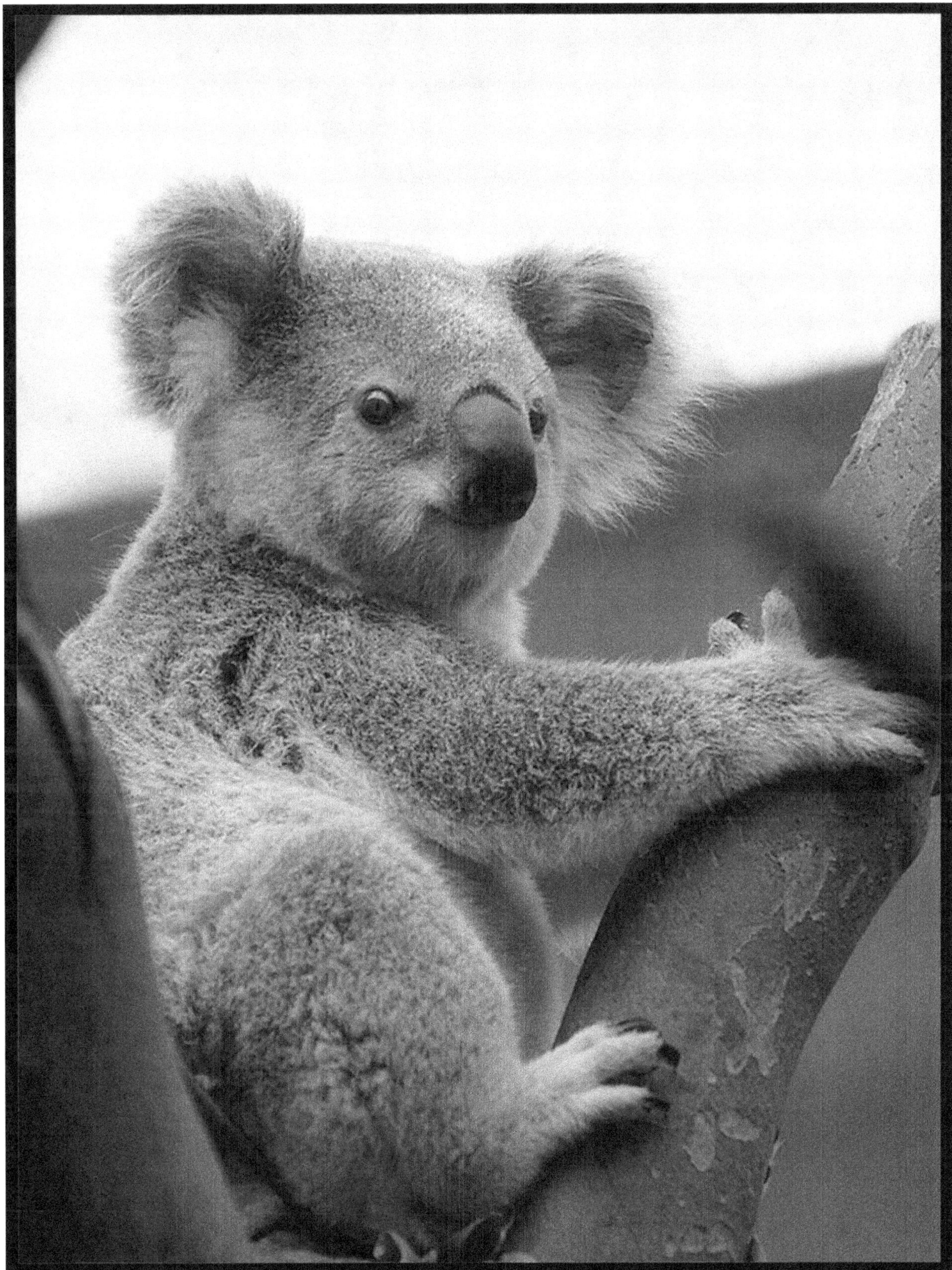

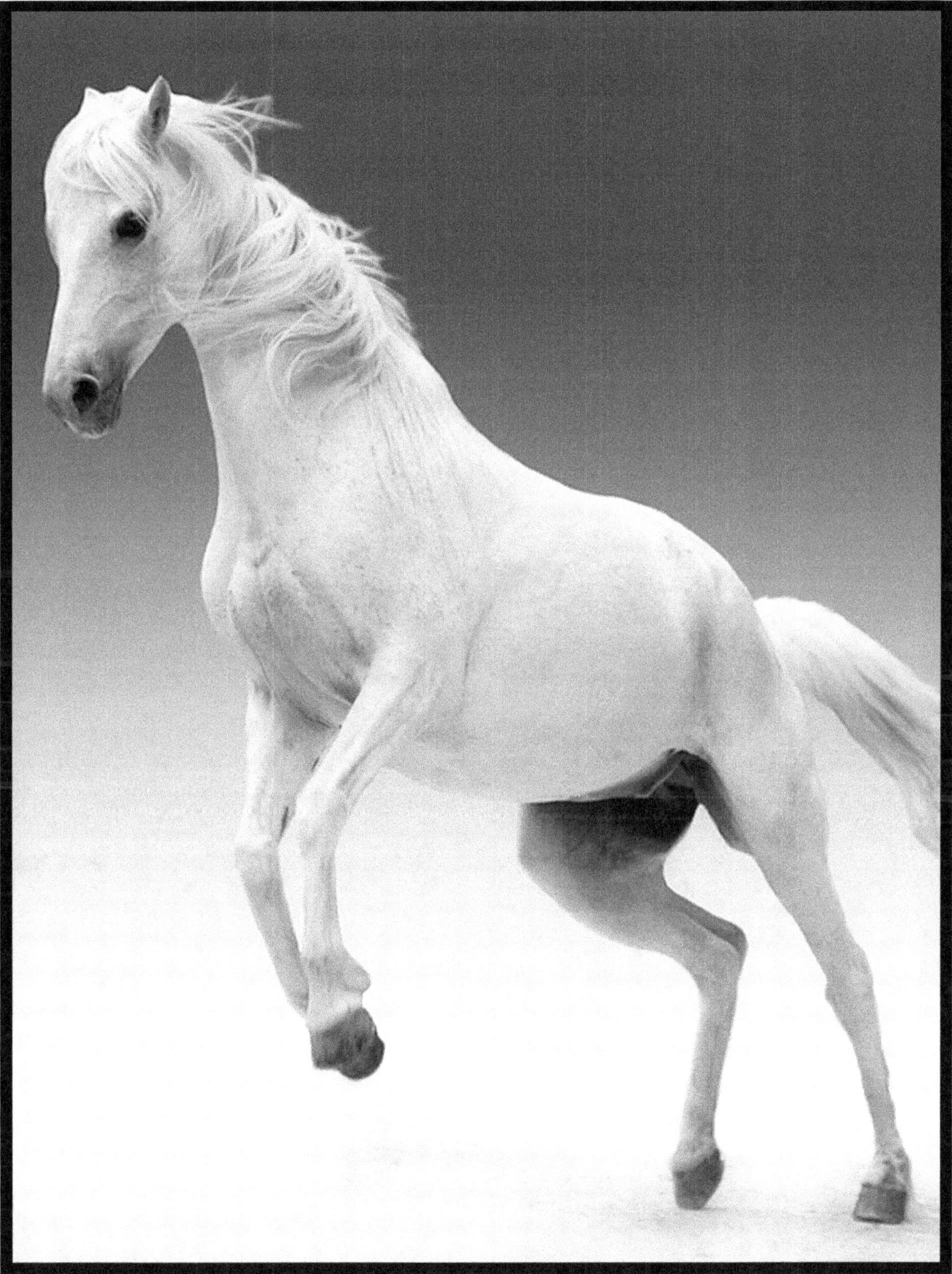

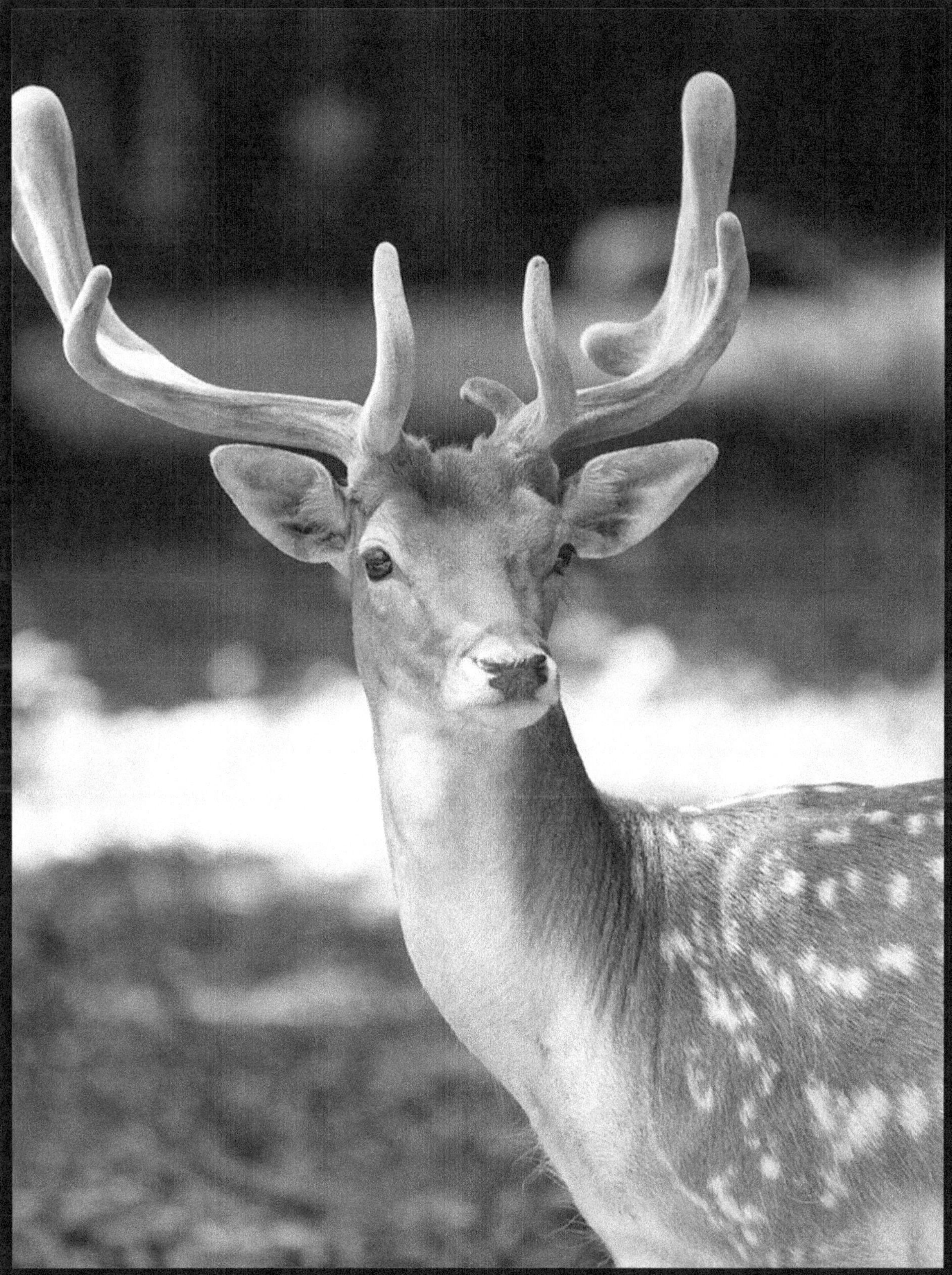

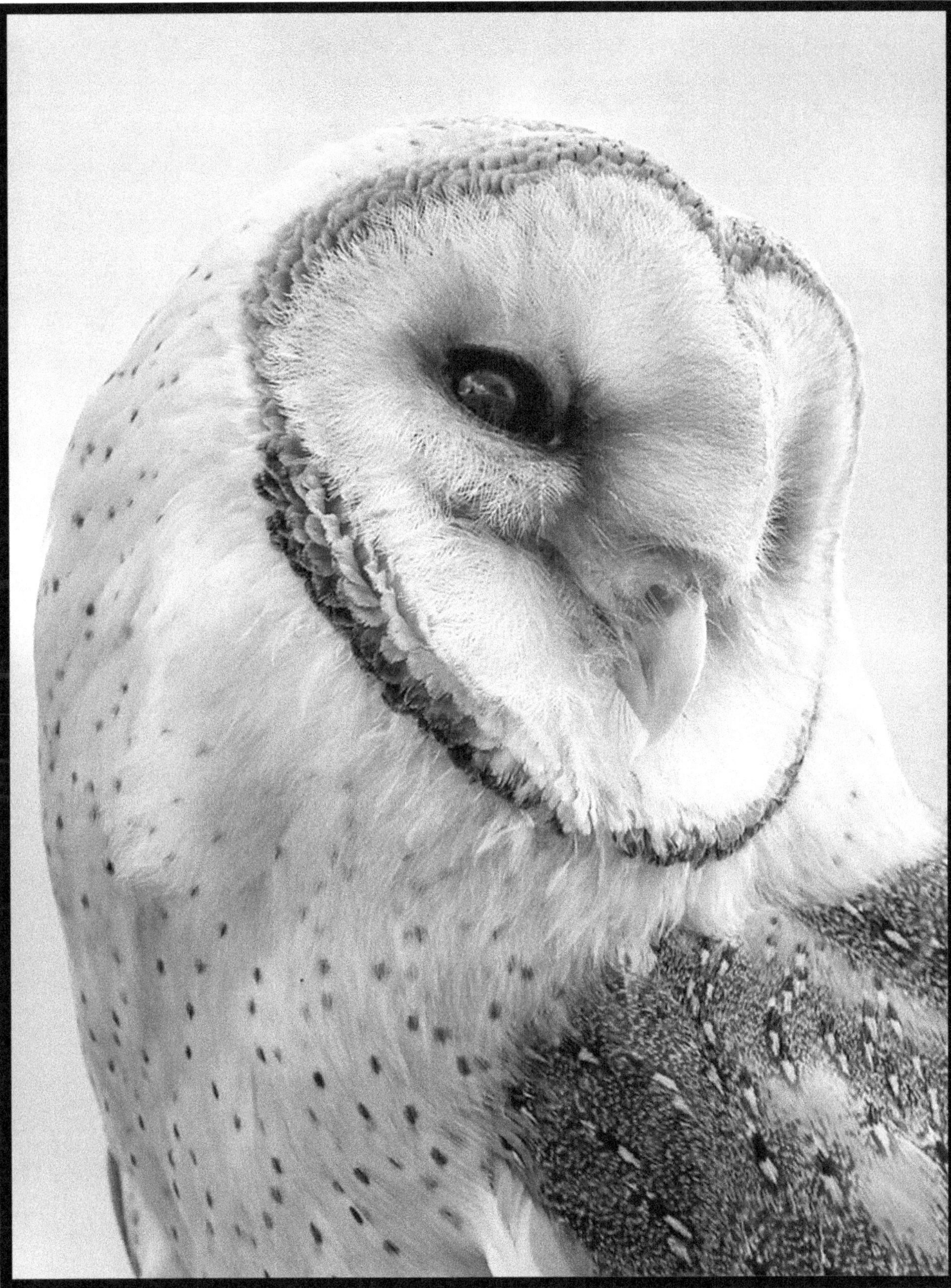

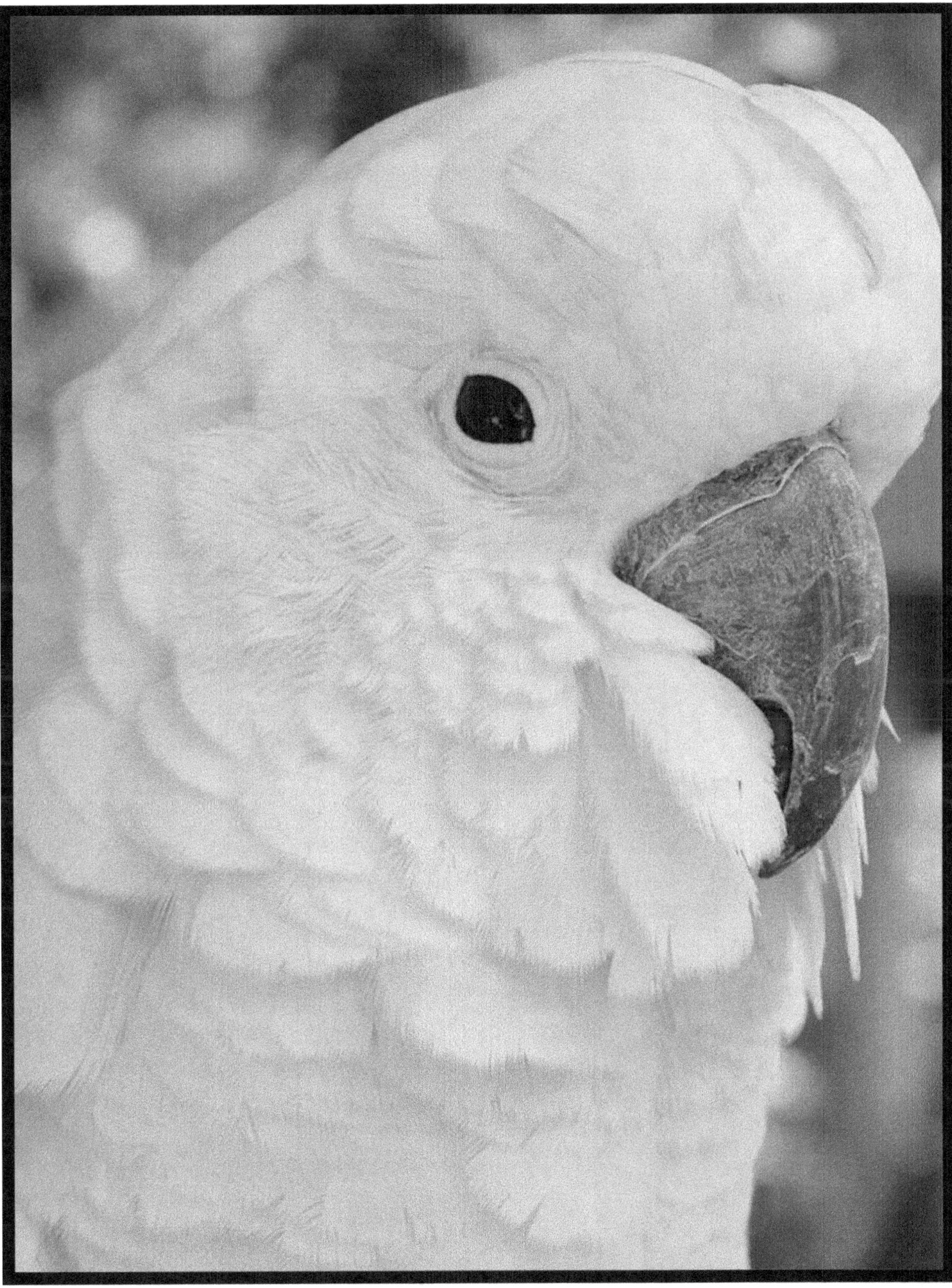

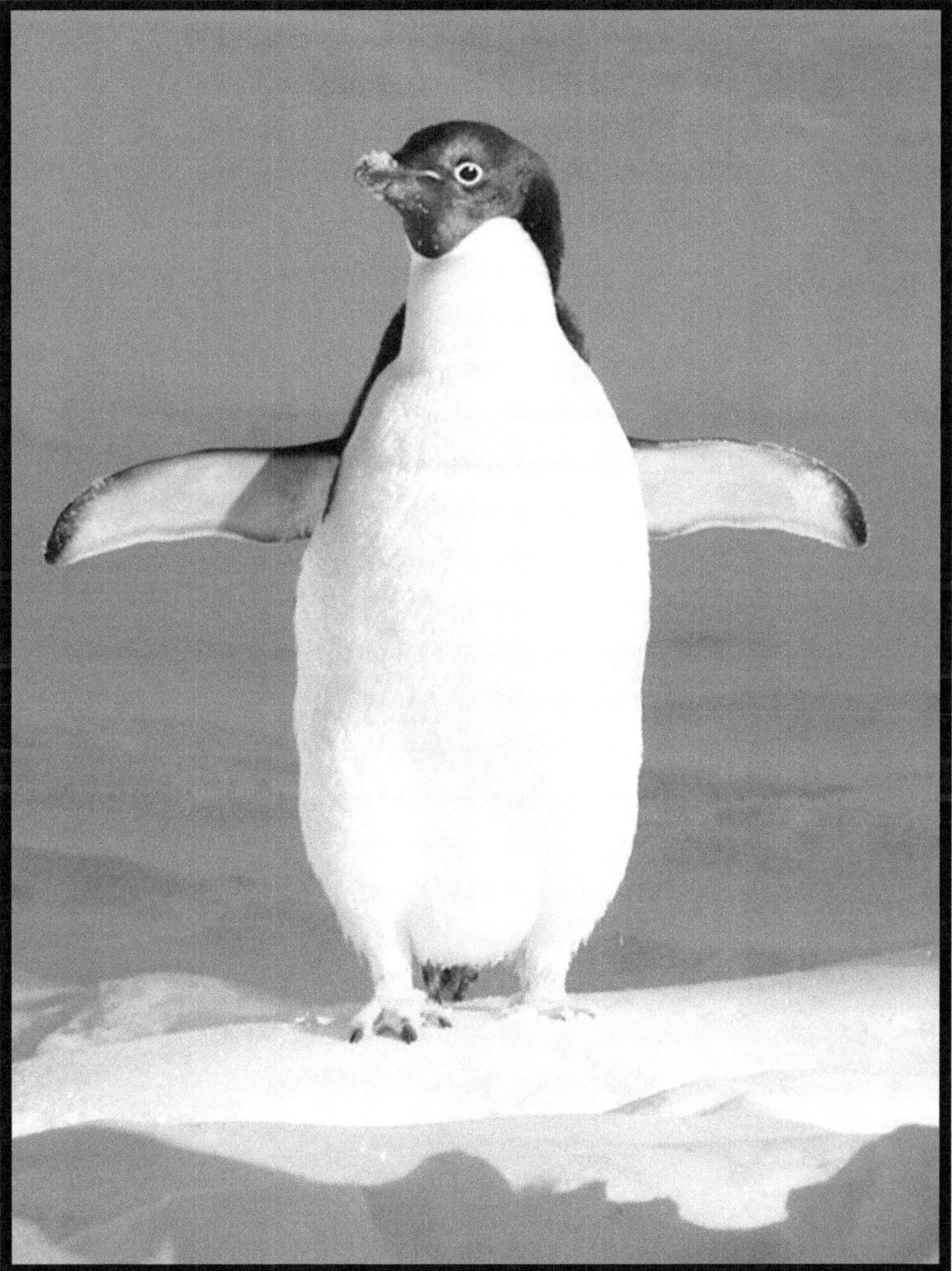

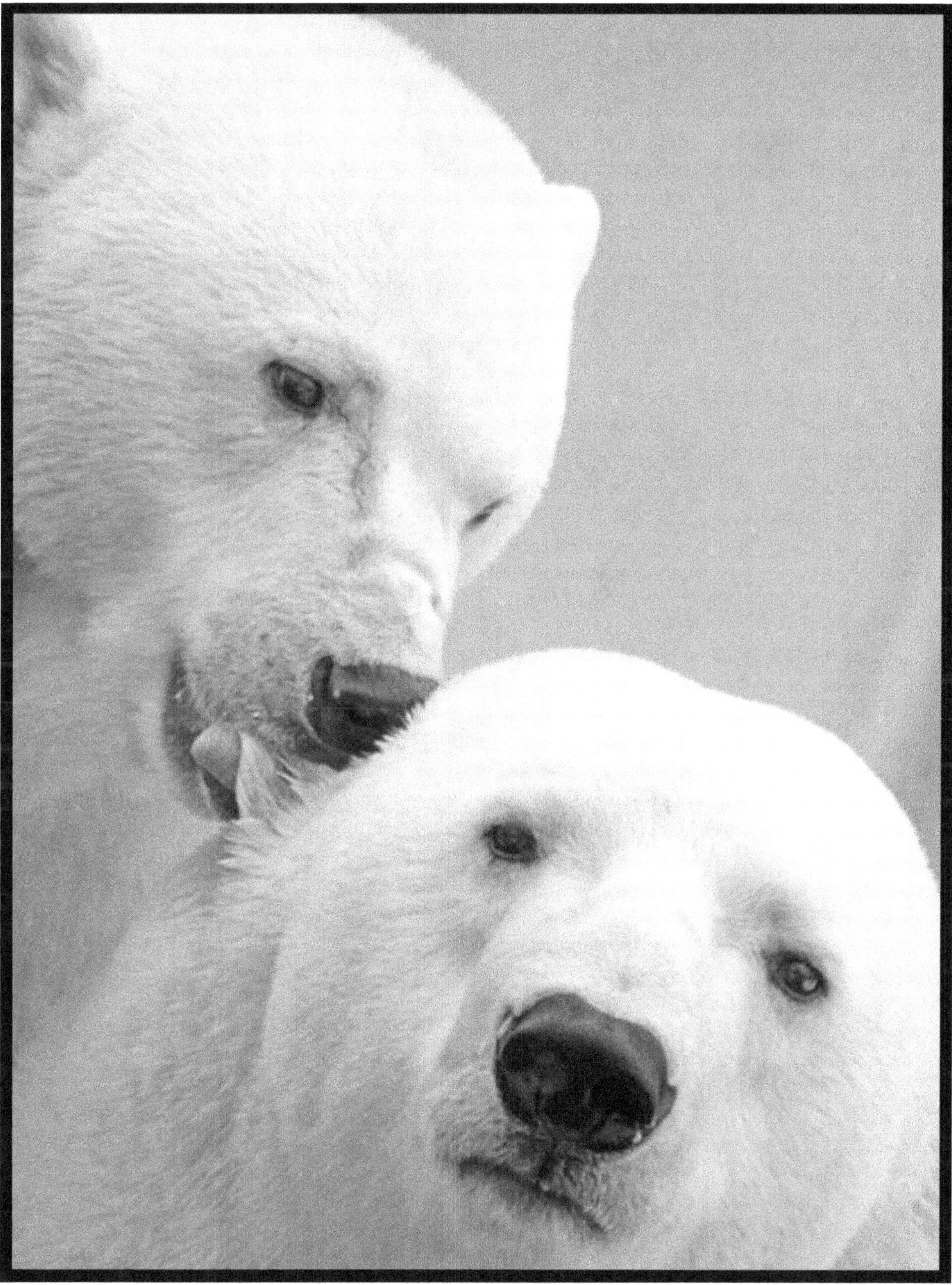

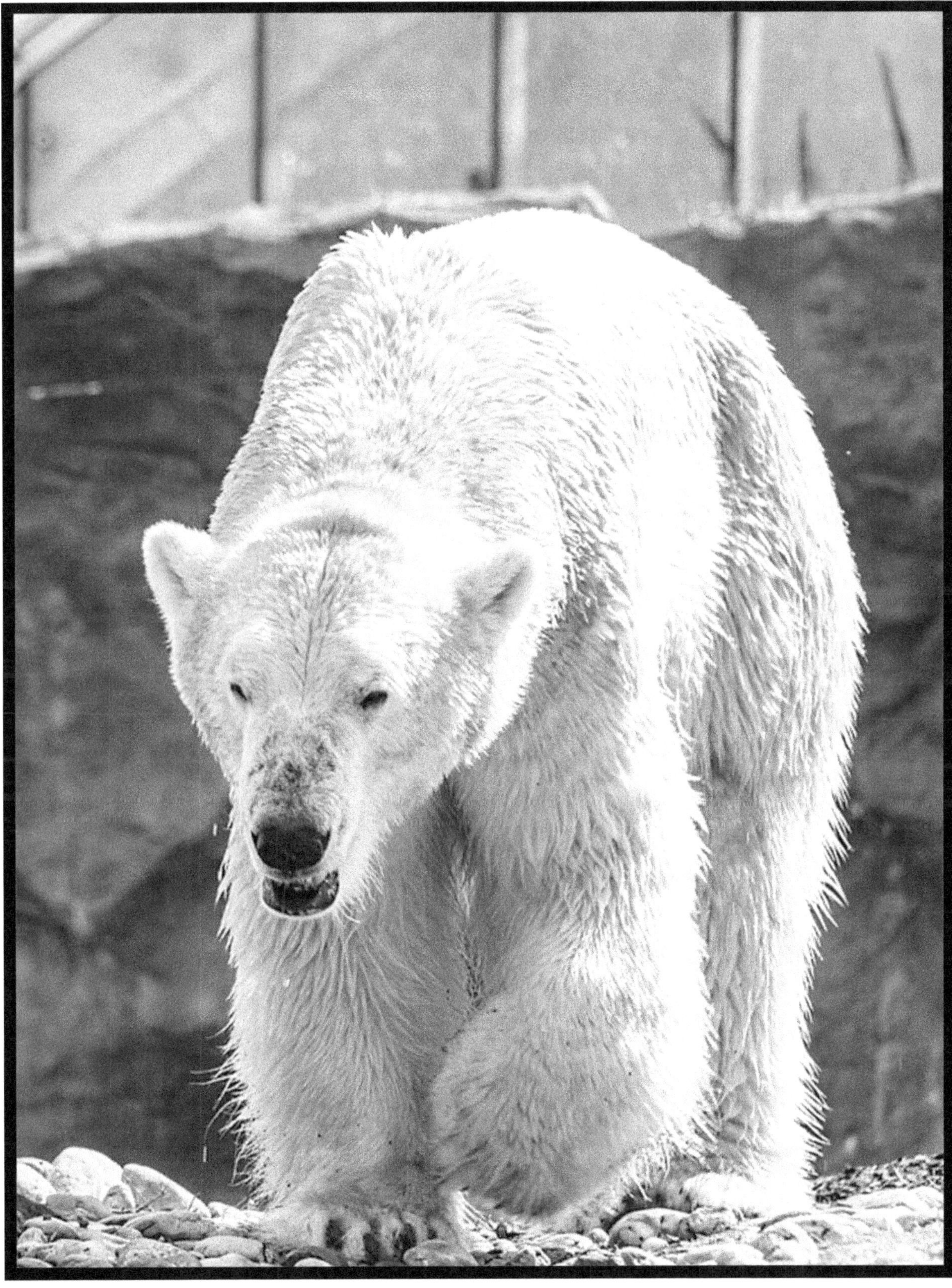

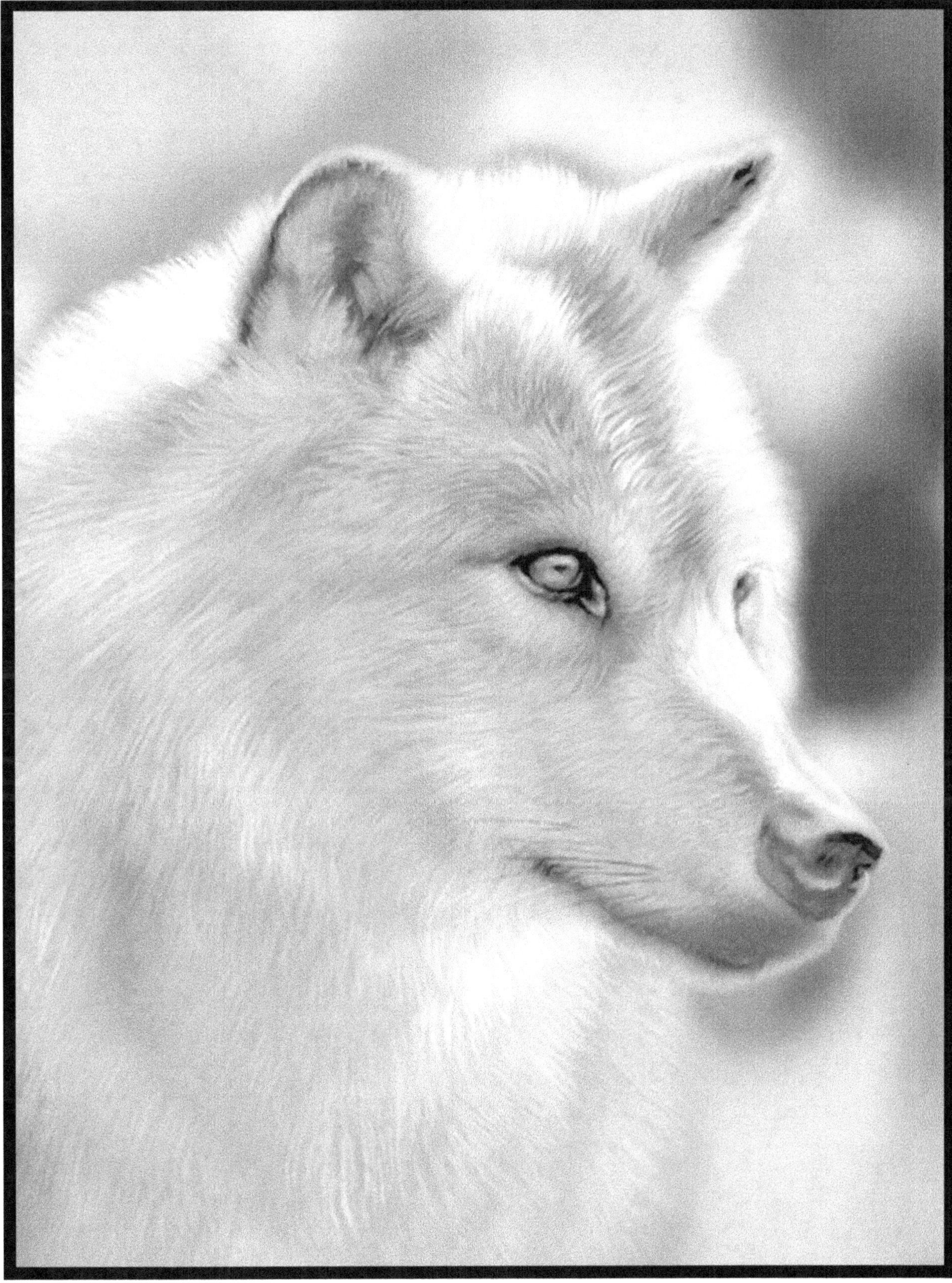

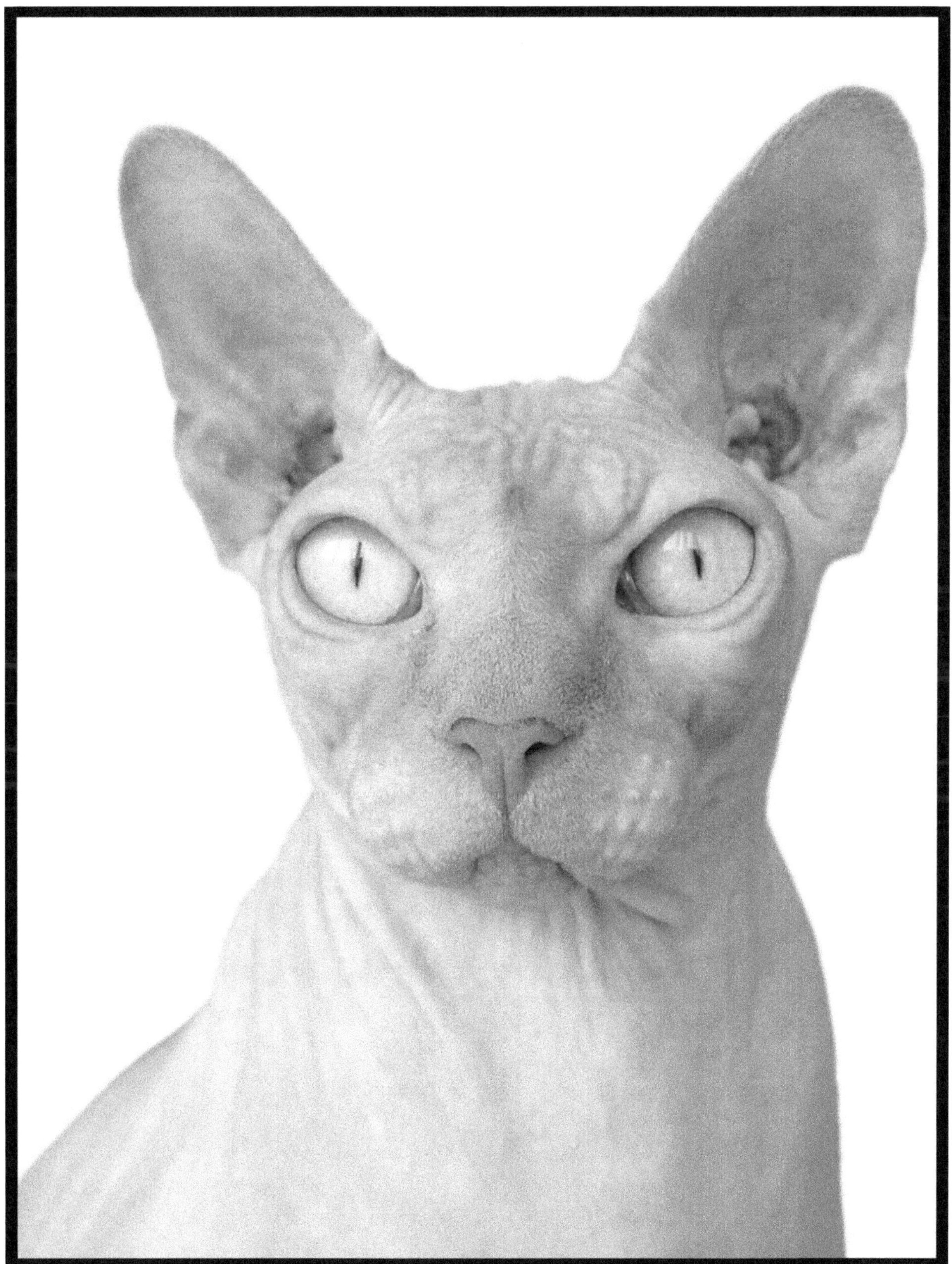

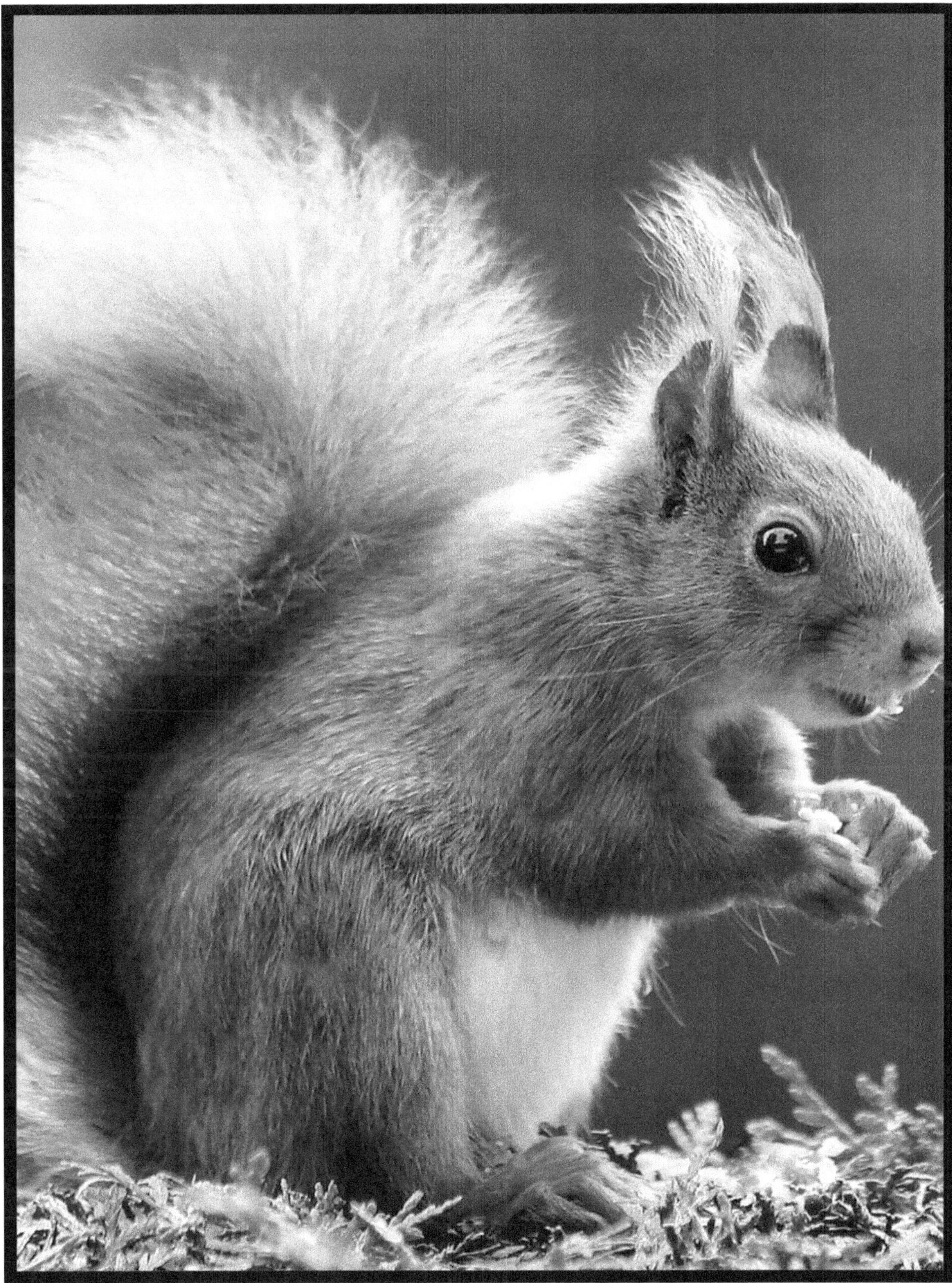

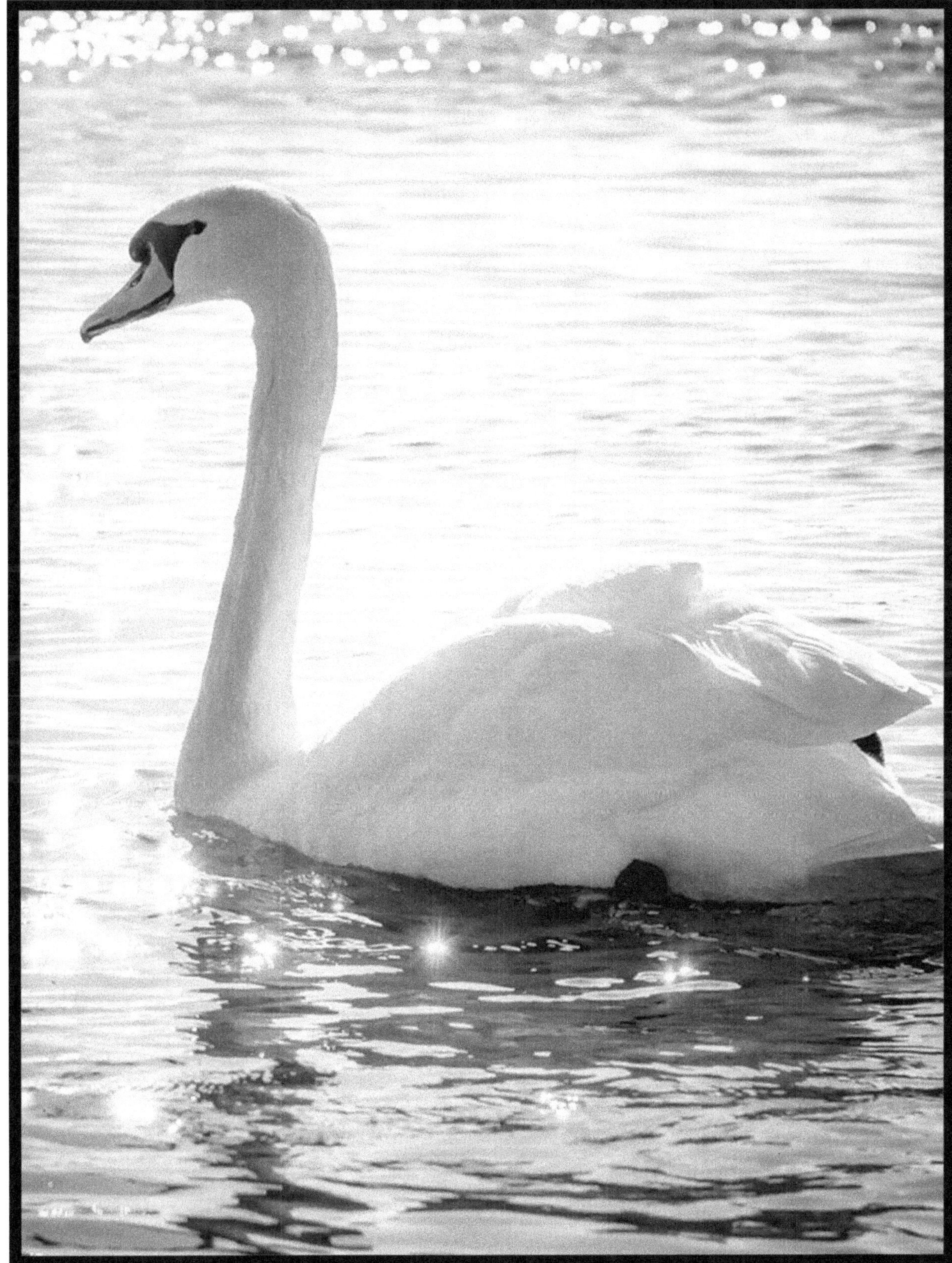

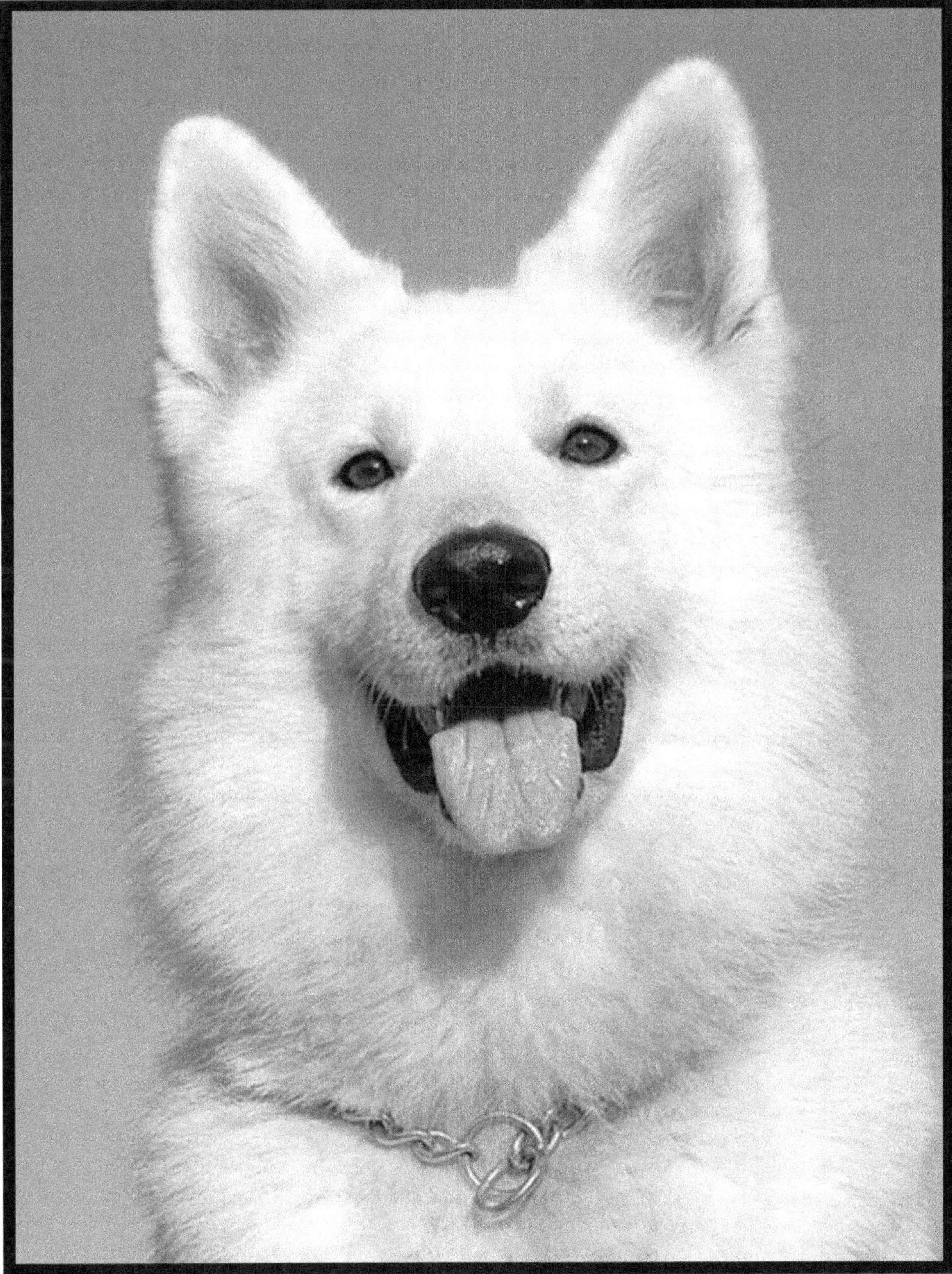

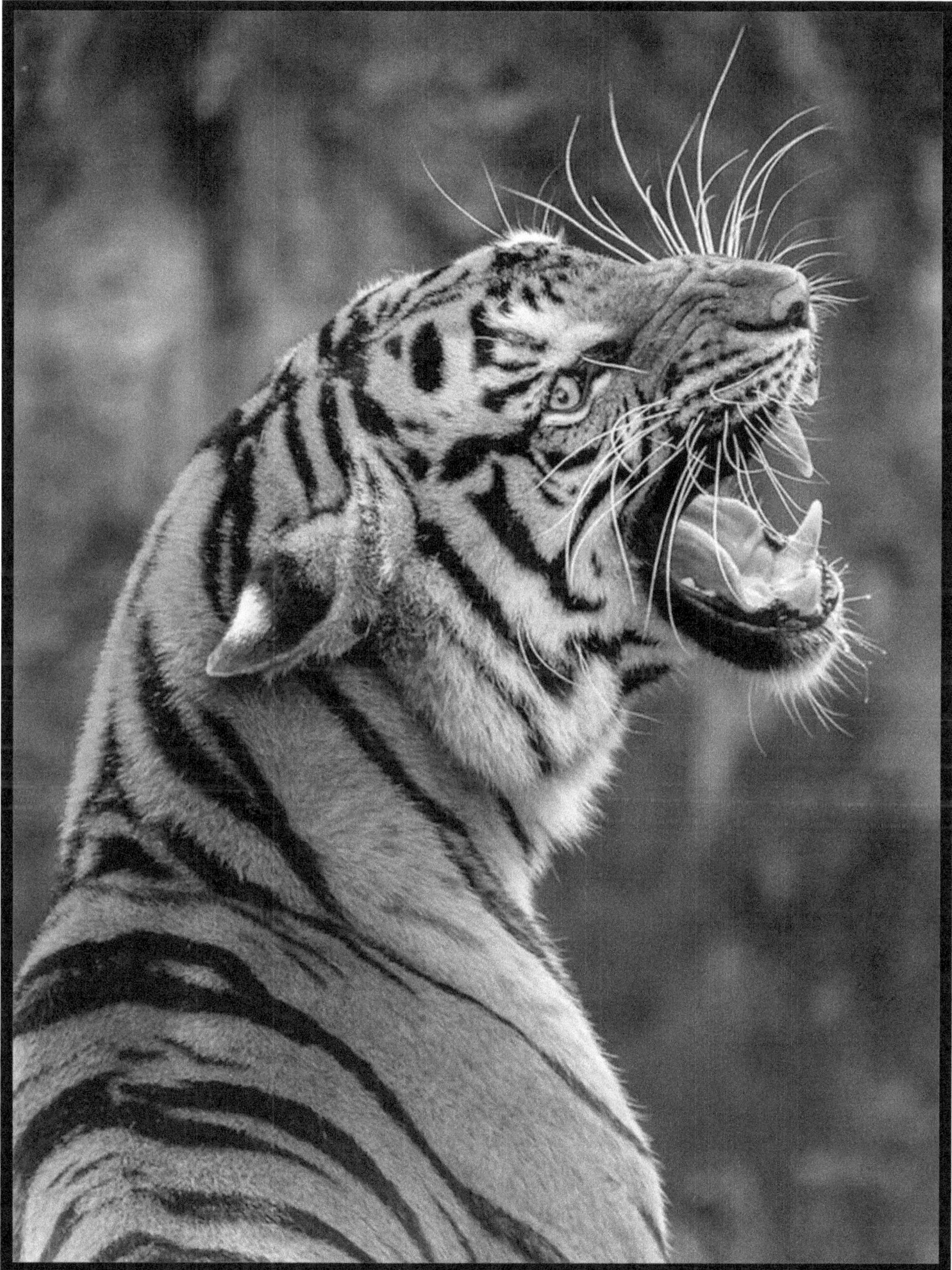

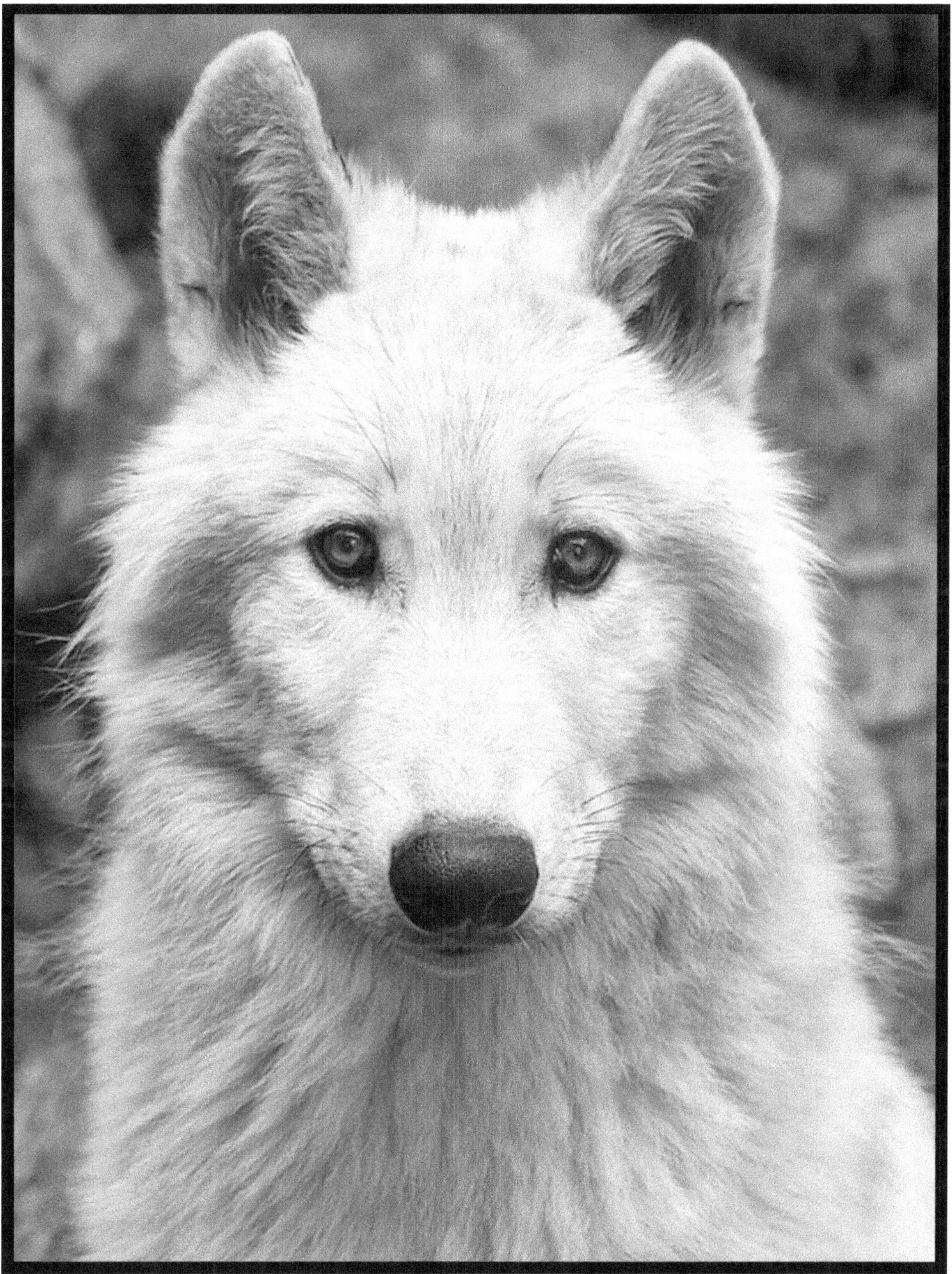

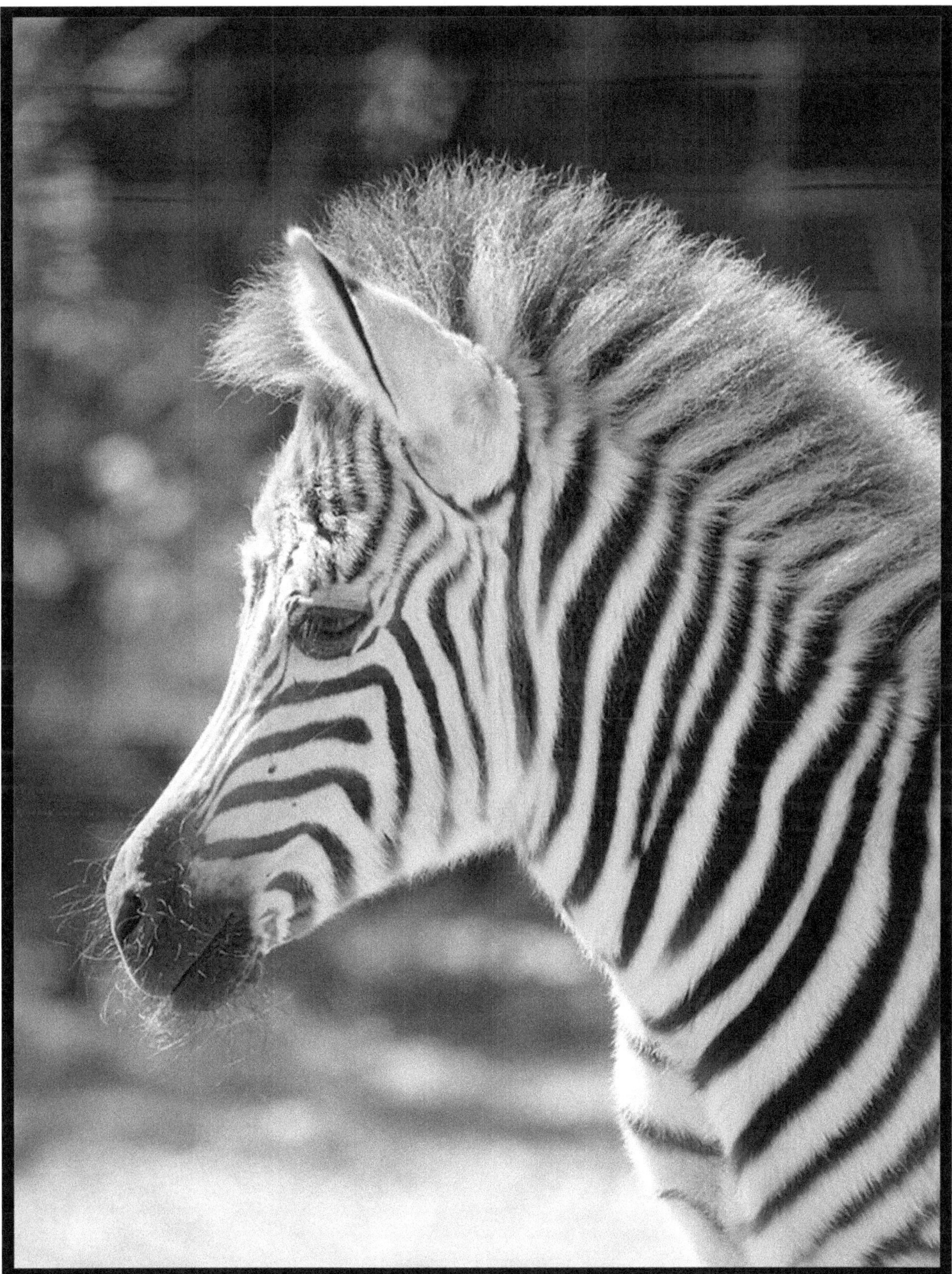

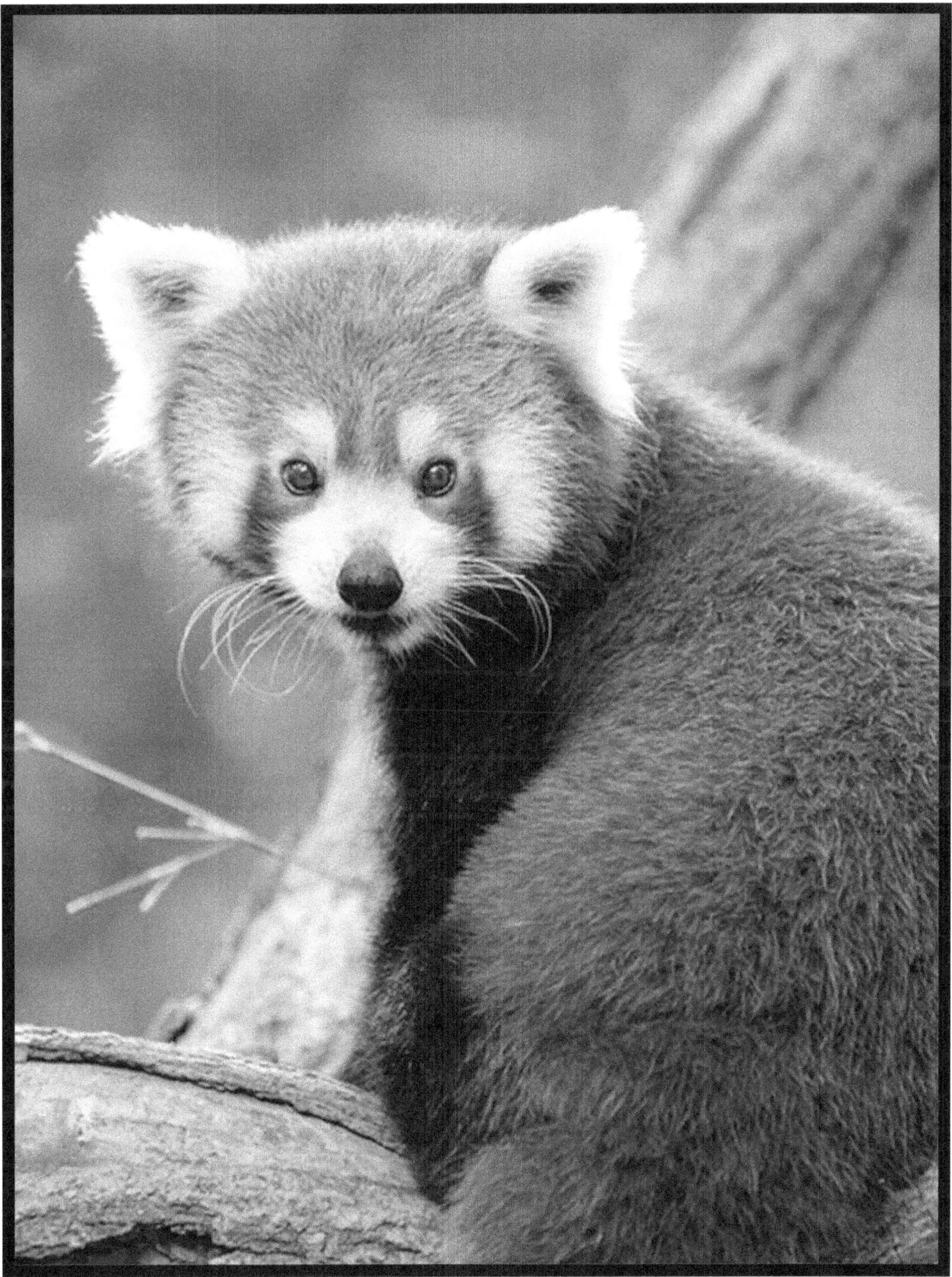

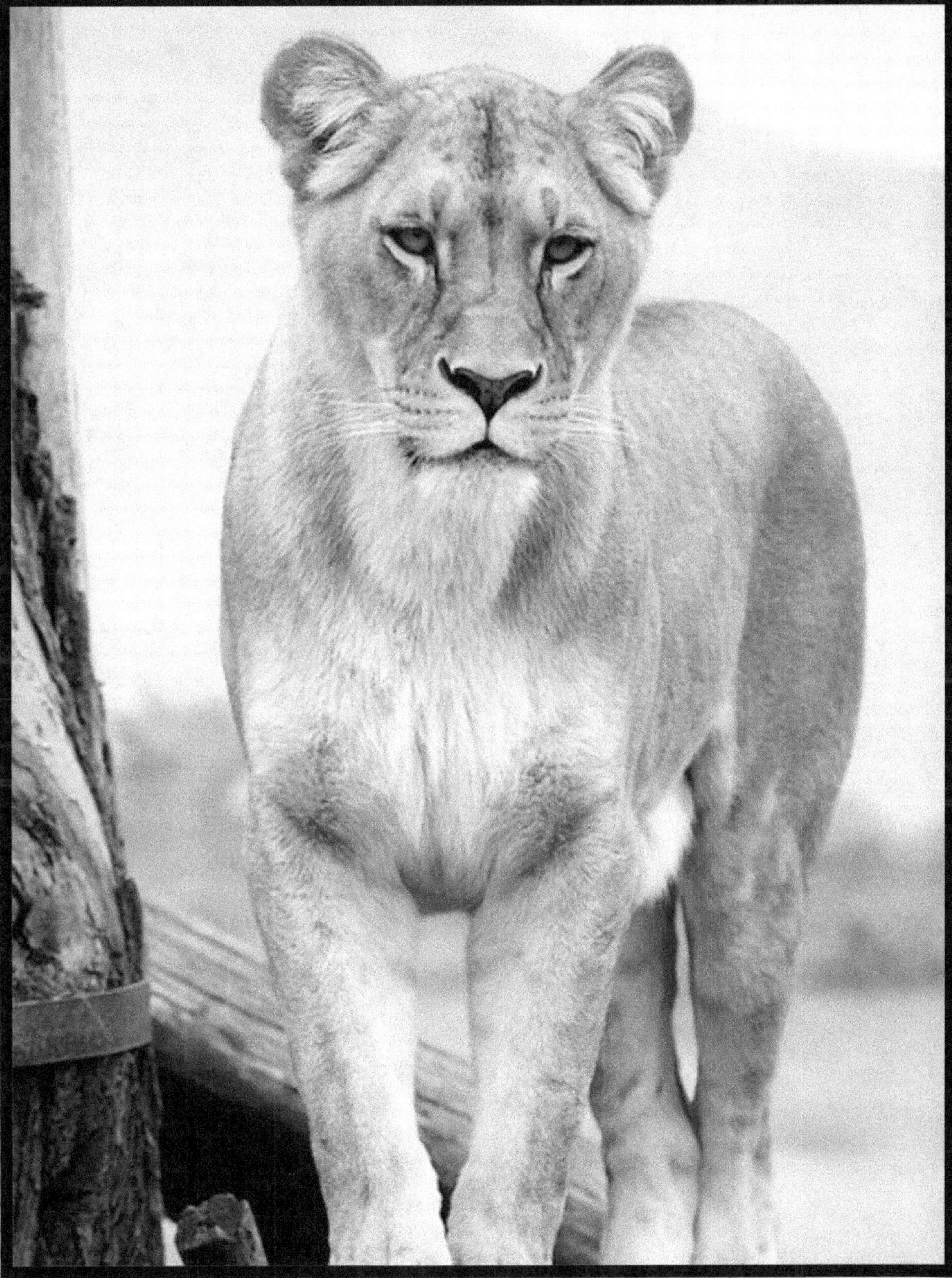

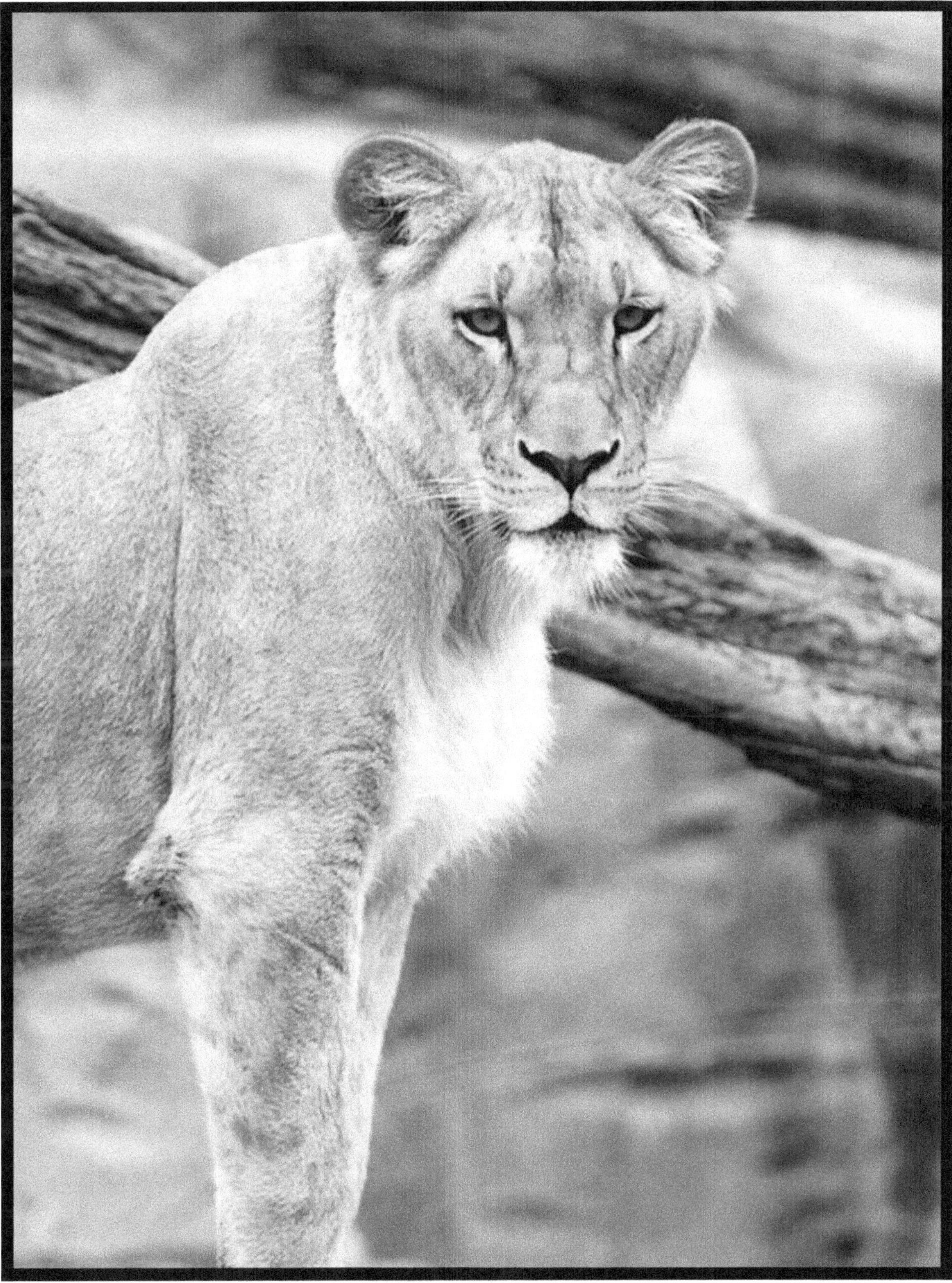

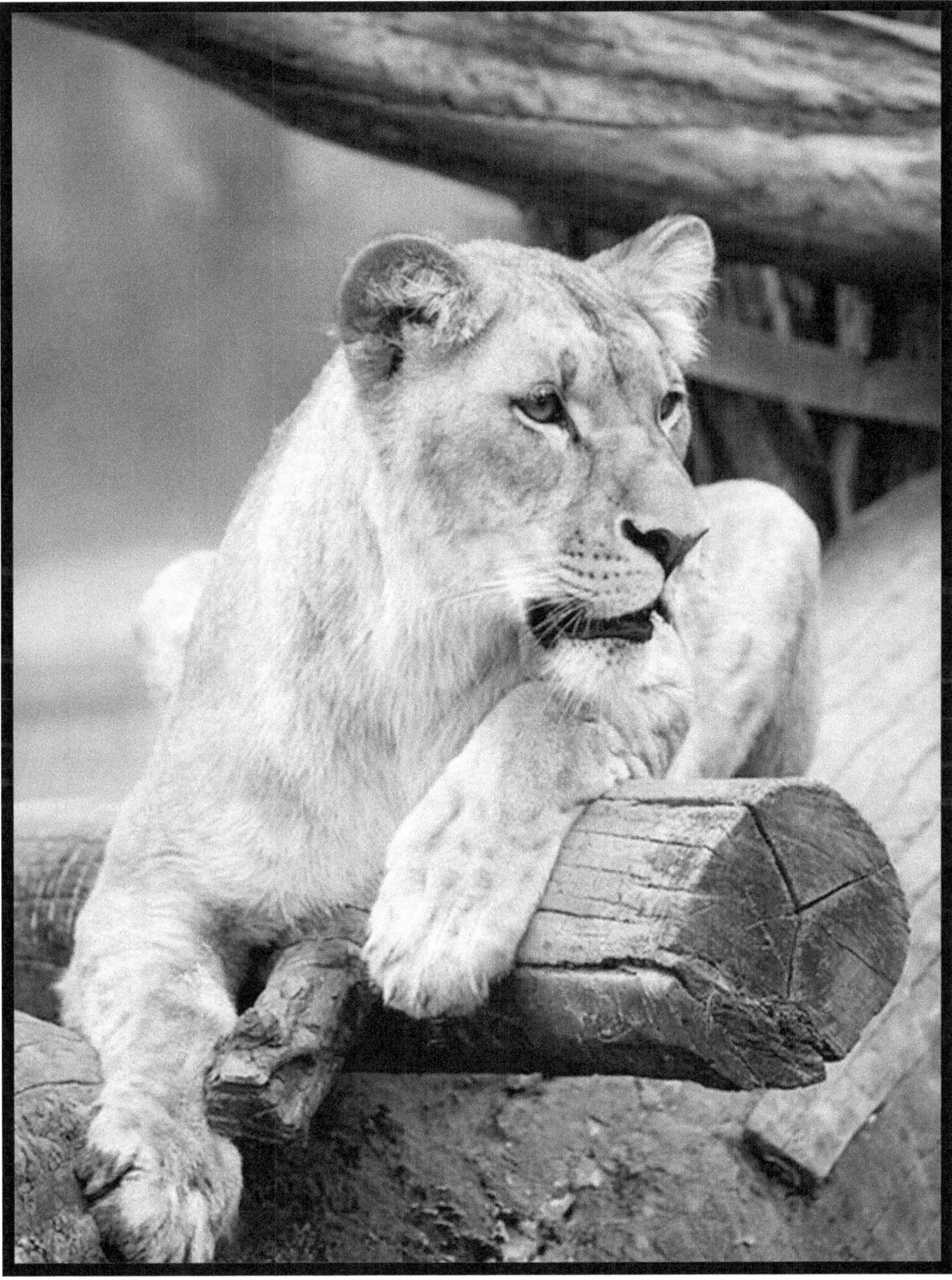

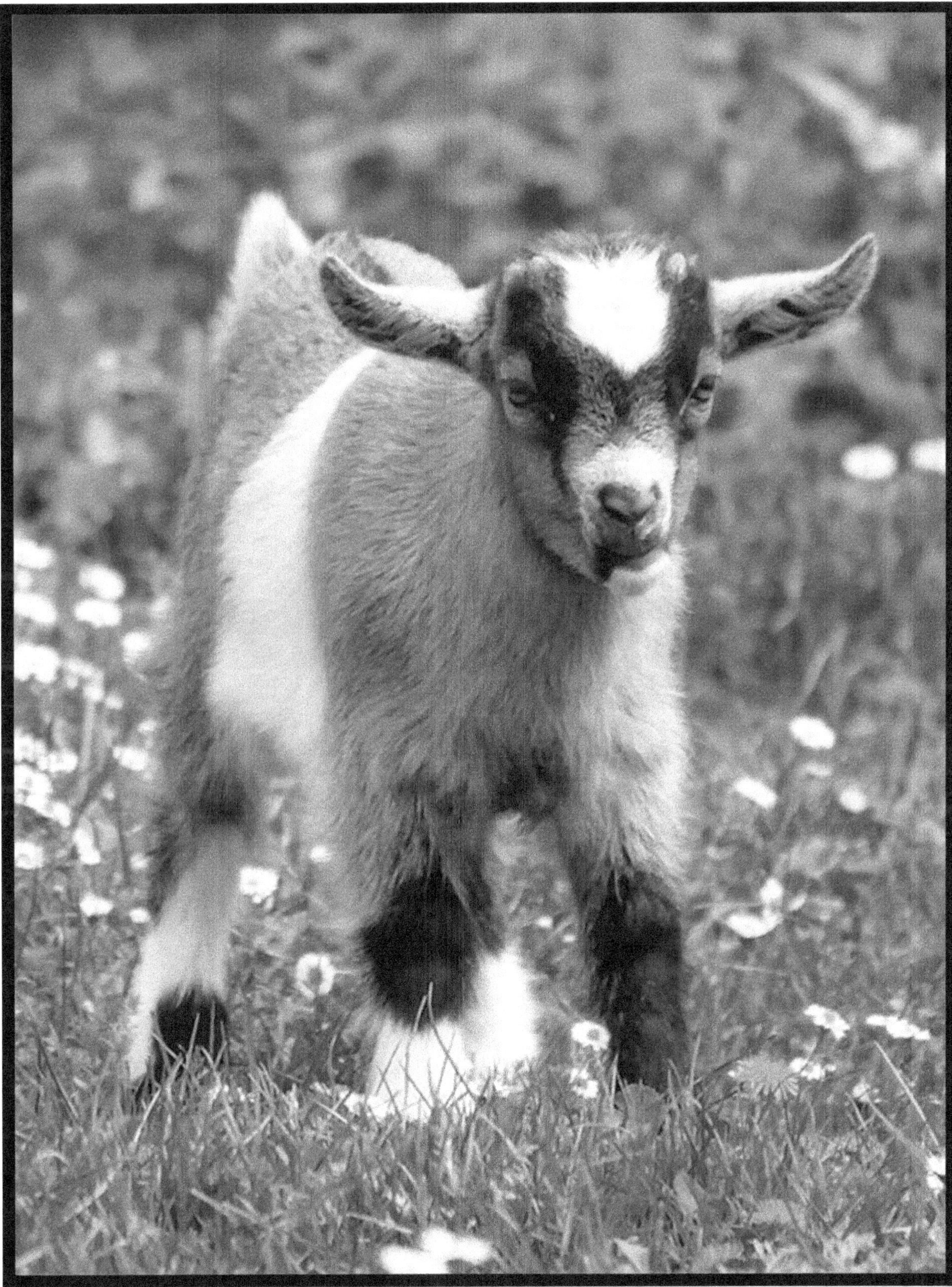

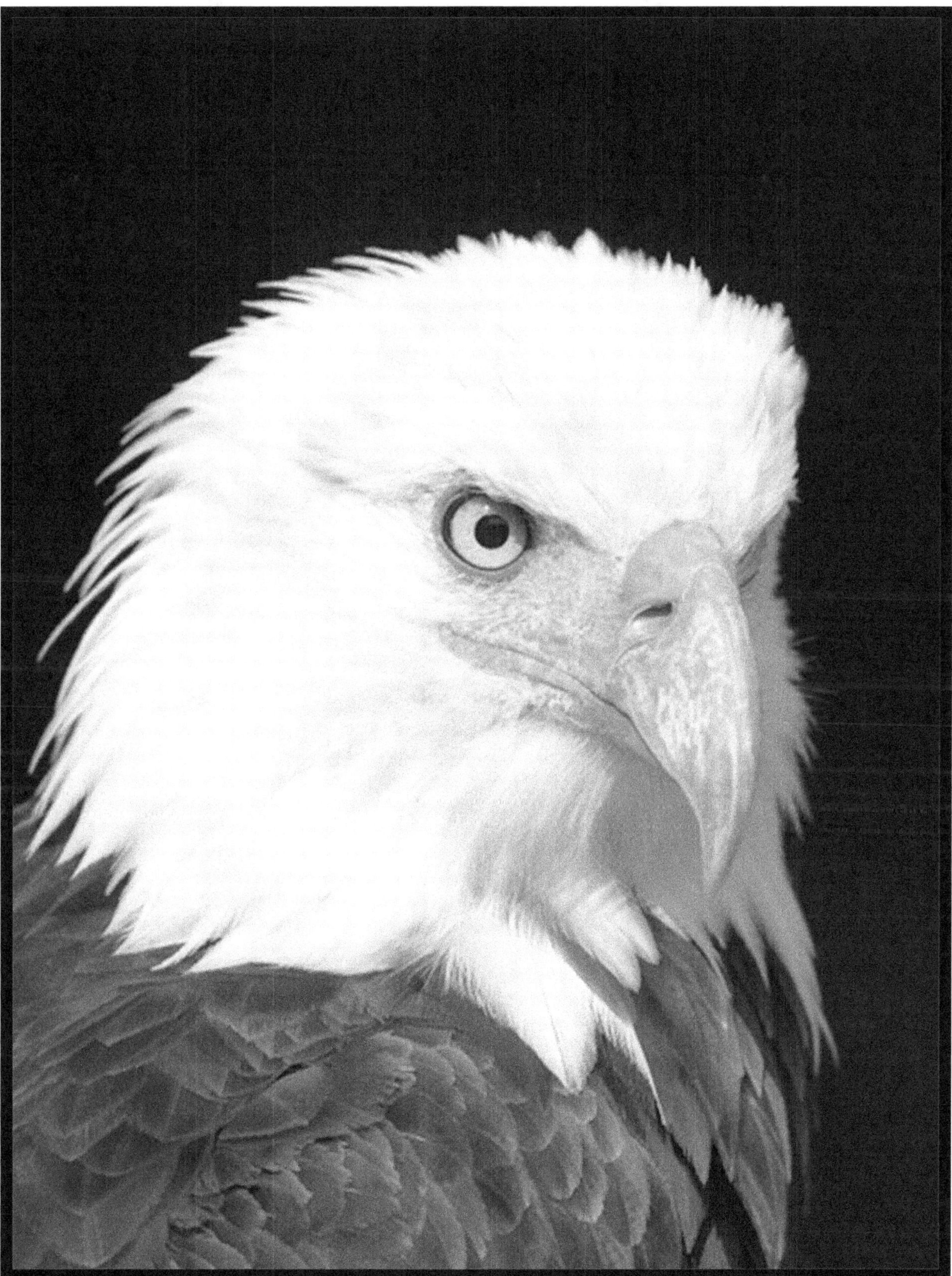